THE CLASSIC
Porsche

THE CLASSIC
Porsche

MIKE McCARTHY

Exeter Books

NEW YORK

A Bison Book

First published in U.S.A.
by Exeter Books
Distributed by Bookthrift
Exeter is a trademark of Bookthrift Marketing, Inc.
Bookthrift is a registered trademark of Bookthrift Marketing, Inc.
New York, New York

ISBN 0-671-07529-2

Printed in Hong Kong

Reprinted 1988

Page 1: The Porsche crest, designed by Ferry Porsche, incorporates the emblem of the city of Stuttgart (the black horse rampant) and the state of Baden-Württemberg (the stylized stags' horns in the background).
Page 2 and 3: The 924, identifiable by the row of intakes and the NACA duct in the hood.
Below: One of the all-time great Porsches, the Type 550 sports/racer.

629.222

Contents

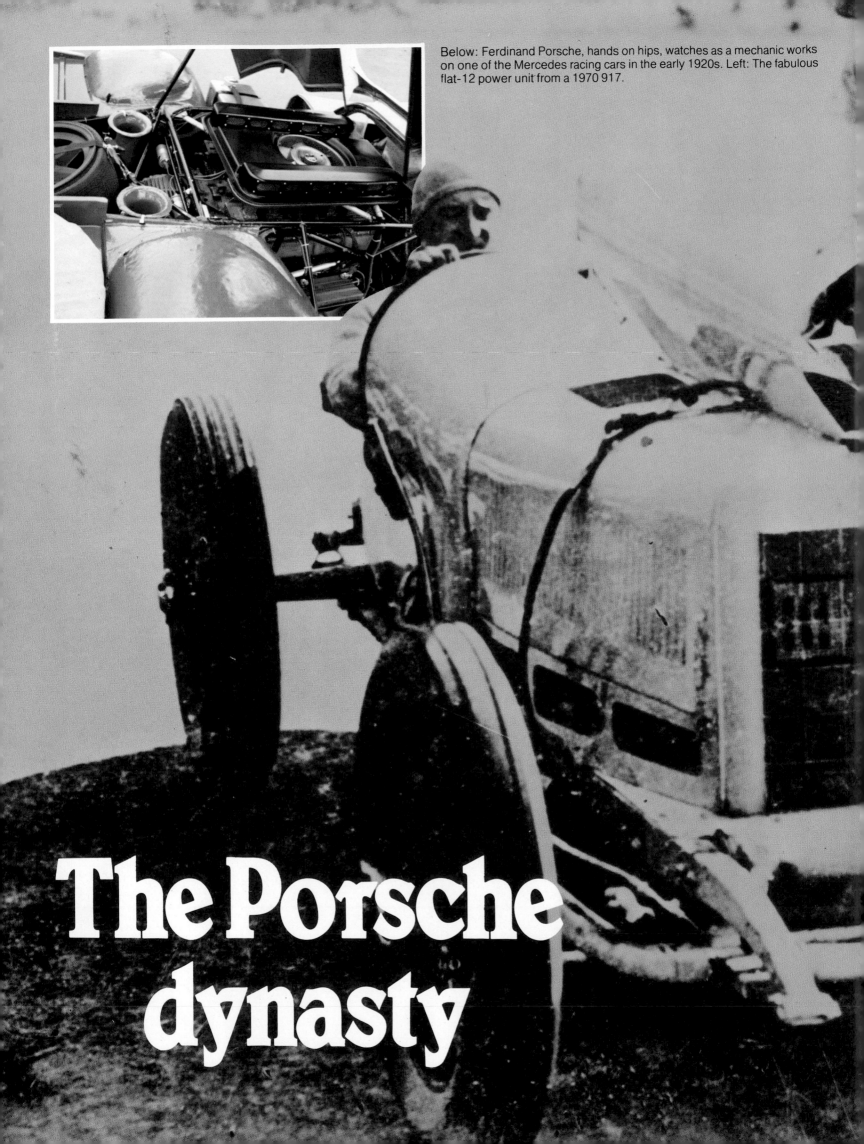

Below: Ferdinand Porsche, hands on hips, watches as a mechanic works on one of the Mercedes racing cars in the early 1920s. Left: The fabulous flat-12 power unit from a 1970 917.

The Porsche dynasty

Ferdinand Anton Porsche was born in 1875 of a Roman Catholic family at Maffersdorf, a town in that most turbulent of political and cultural areas, Bohemia, which at the time was part of the Austro-Hungarian Empire.

He seems to have been a precocious youngster, fitting new-fangled electric lighting to his father's house while still a teenager. He upset his father by going to a technical college, where he received a rudimentary but solid education, rather than joining the family tinsmiths shop.

He served an apprenticeship at an electrical firm in Vienna, and then at 23 years of age joined a company called Lohner. They were carriage-makers turned automobile manufacturers, making electrically-powered machines under license from the French Jeantaud firm: his electrical background thus came in useful.

Two years after joining Lohner, in 1900, when he was just 25 years old, the first of the cars to bear his name appeared: the Lohner-Porsche. Young Porsche's ideas were revolutionary. In the Lohner-Porsche the batteries drove the front wheels via hub-mounted motors.

His next design was yet more brilliant. Since the batteries accounted for most of the weight of electric cars, he did away with them. In 1902 he introduced the Lohner-Porsche *Mixte* system, wherein a petrol engine drove a generator, which in turn drove the wheel-mounted motors.

Even at this stage Porsche was a great racing enthusiast. He competed in both the ordinary electric car and one of the *Mixte* machines, gaining successes with both. In fact the *Mixte* arrangement was exceedingly versatile: during World War One he designed a successful land train for the Austrian army.

In 1905 Porsche was appointed technical head of Austro-Daimler. Here over the years, he was responsible for the Prince Henry model, an air-cooled flat-four aero engine and in 1921 the delightful little Sascha racing car, which achieved some success in the Targa Florio, driven by the legendary Alfred Neubauer. One of his mechanics later became even more famous than either Porsche or Neubauer — we know him today as Marshal Tito.

In 1916 Porsche was appointed Managing Director of Austro-Daimler: he received the Officer's Cross of Franz Joseph for his work on behalf of the war effort; and he was awarded an honorary doctorate by the Technische Hochschule of Vienna.

Long before this Porsche had married Aloisia Johanna Kaes, and had fathered two children — Louise in 1904 and in 1909 Ferdinand Anton Ernst, first nicknamed 'Ferdy,' later altered to 'Ferry.'

By 1923 Dr Porsche, always more interested in matters technical than financial, was at loggerheads with the backers of Austro-Daimler. He comes across as a man of blunt manners. This was to lead to many partings of the ways, but in this instance he joined a distant cousin company of Austro-Daimler, the Daimler Motoren Gesellschaft in Stuttgart, as Technical Director. Under his guidance a series of supercharged sports and racing cars began to appear, culminating in the magnificent SS, SSK and SSKL machines.

In spite of his prolific output, his time at Daimler was not very happy. A number of factors contributed to this, but probably the most significant was the merger between Daimler and Benz to form Daimler-Benz. Infighting between the two factions broke out, though on the whole it was the Porsche designs that won the day. Matters didn't improve when the Germans wouldn't recognize his honorary Doctorate of Engineering from Vienna — though they hastily re-awarded him the same title from the Stuttgart Technische

Right: Anton Piëch stands beside the first Gmünd-built coupe, and the second-ever Porsche. Note the curved front quarter lights and unusual rear end treatment. (Piëch was Ferdinand Porsche's brother-in-law.)

Below: Three generations of Porsche. Dr Ferdinand is flanked by son Ferry on the left and grandson Peter on the right.

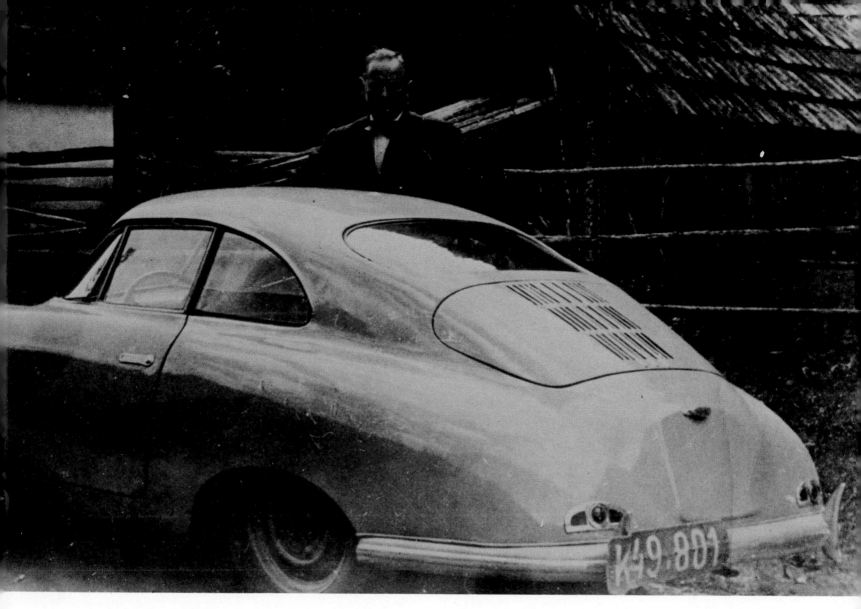

Hochschule when a Porsche-designed Mercedes won the Targa Florio in 1924.

While he was at Daimler-Benz, incidentally, he came into contact with a car that was to be one of the pointers to the future – the Benz *Tropfenwagen*. This was the famous Rumpler-designed, teardrop-shaped, mid-engined racer which, though startling to look at, was not successful as it was underpowered. In 1928, however, when his contract came up for renewal, the company made Porsche an offer calculated to insult: there was no alternative but to leave.

Porsche then moved back to Austria, in 1929, to the Steyr group, as Chief Engineer. He designed for them the small Type 30, taking nine months from initial design to running prototype, and the larger Austria – which featured swing axles at the rear. However, his chair barely had time to become warm when another of those quirks of fate overtook him. Austro-Daimler bought out Steyr! As he was *persona non grata* at Austro-Daimler, they rescinded his three-year contract after only one year. Where next?

All his life Porsche had worked for others, some of whom had made considerably more profit from his designs than he himself. By this time Porsche was 54, and tired of company politics. In spite of a couple of tempting offers, Porsche decided to set up an independent consulting business, an idea that he had in fact been considering for some time. Thus it was that, by 1931, the Porsche Konstruktionbüro für Motoren-Fahrzeug-Luftfahrzeug und Wasserfahrzeugbau was established. As the name indicates, the company would take on anything that moved on land, sea or in the air, and even such machinery as stationary power plants.

Germany in the late 1920s and early 1930s was a difficult place in which to start up a new operation, due to runaway inflation.

The Porsche company's first outside contract, to design a small 2-liter car for the Wanderer concern, was arbitrarily given the project number 'Type 7' – they did not want anyone to think that this was the first from the newly-constituted company! Of much more significance was another early project, the Type 12. The brief came from the Zündapp firm of motorcycle manufacturers: two-wheeler sales were slumping, so the head of Zündapp, Neumeyer, approached Porsche to design for him a small, cheap car that Zündapp could use to bridge the current economic climate.

The Type 12 was decidedly different. For a start the engine was a 1.2-liter five-cylinder radial, water-cooled, mounted at the back of a backbone chassis, with independent suspension all round via transverse leaf springs and semi-leading and trailing arms. It was clothed in a 'streamlined' body.

And then, as production was about to begin, motorcycle sales had started to boom and there was no time and effort at Zündapp to start making cars.

During 1932 Porsche had won another contract, to design yet again a 'small, inexpensive' car for another motorcycle manufacturer, NSU. It was to have a four-cylinder air-cooled engine in the tail, independent suspension all round but this time via torsion bars, and a chassis consisting of a central backbone with sheet metal panels outrigged on either side. Again the mechanicals were enclosed in a streamlined body which bore a striking resemblance to what would

Left: Anton Piëch on the left and Ferry Porsche on the right with the first Gmünd-built 356 coupe. Right: Inside the Gmünd factory (little more than a woodshed) one of the first aluminum bodies is hand finished.

later appear as the Volkswagen. The Type 32 could accurately be called the forerunner of the Beetle . . . But, as before, the NSU project was dropped.

Almost as a sideline, the Porsche company in 1932 had started designing a single seater Grand Prix car for the new formula, which only set a minimum weight limit at 750kg, or about 1650lb. The proposed power plant was a V16 with a novel form of valve gear. It was complex but did work, because from an initial 240 to 250bhp from 4.5 liters, the output rose to no less than 600bhp from 6 liters.

Far more radical, however, was the general layout of the car. The engine was placed amidships with the gearbox behind the rear axle centre line. The driver sat in the nose, with the petrol tank between him and the engine. Torsion bar suspension was used; Erwin Komenda's sleek, light bodywork fitted snugly around the mechanicals — and even used doped fabric for some of the panels. The chassis was a tubular affair, the long side members acting also as coolant pipes, taking water from the engine to the front-mounted radiator.

Contrary to popular opinion, Ferry Porsche claims responsibility for the engine location. But, no doubt, the shadow of the Tropfenwagen was lingering somewhere. One reason for the configuration that Ferry Porsche gives is that it optimized the power to weight ratio, though this could be questioned on the grounds that Daimler-Benz achieved similar results with a more conventional layout. Another reason was that, since the petrol tank was located at the center of gravity, the handling characteristics of the car stayed constant. This may have been true, but what is equally true is that the handling was constantly tricky as well, and required very brave and incredibly skilled drivers to get the best out of the cars. The mid-engine set up was, of course, to become the standard for all Formula 1 cars some two decades later, but, to be honest, this was more due to the influence of Cooper than Porsche.

Reverting back to 1933, when Hitler announced his grandiose plans for state sponsorship of a Grand Prix car,

Daimler-Benz thought they alone would build it. Porsche approached the newly-formed Auto Union combine, the result of a merger between Horch, DKW, Audi and Wanderer, and offered them the Type 22. They liked the idea, but there was a condition — that they receive some of the 600,000 mark sponsorship.

In March 1933 Dr Porsche was one of a delegation from Auto Union to Hitler to sell him the Auto Union Grand Prix car. By coincidence Hitler had met Porsche in 1925 at a race meeting at Solitude: Porsche had forgotten, but Hitler had not. The fact that they were both Austrian born may have helped, as would the fact that most of the paperwork had been done. Hitler split the 600,000 marks. The Type 22, the Auto Union GP car, was off and running. Along with Mercedes-Benz they were to dominate prewar racing, much to Hitler's delight.

In January 1934 Hitler opened the Berlin Motor Show, and in his speech propounded the idea of a mass-produced car, simple, reliable, economical, which anyone who could afford a motorcycle could also buy. 'A real people's car — a sort of *Volkswagen*. . .'.

In May that year Hitler and Porsche, along with Hitler's adviser on matters automotive, Jallob Werlin, met again, to thrash out the technical aspects of the Volkswagen. It now appears that the whole Volkswagen concept and organization to go with it were mapped out as well at that meeting.

Since time and money were short, the three prototypes were built in the garage of Porsche's house on Feuerbacher Weg. Once the VW ball was rolling, however, it gathered more and more momentum, albeit in a cumbersome way, so that the program grew rather protracted, and the Porsches at times found life an uphill struggle. For example, a whispering campaign was started to discredit Dr Porsche by pointing out that he was not a German, but a Czech. Hitler merely shrugged and, a couple of weeks later, Dr Porsche was told that he and his family were Germans. It was his turn to shrug — there was nothing he could do about it!

As the 1930s drew to a close, Professor Porsche found

himself more and more involved in the VW project, designing the Wolfsburg plant and becoming a director of the operation. In spite of this he still had time to concern himself with many of the other Porsche design office schemes and contracts, from a volks-tractor to a multitude of VW variants.

The 1930s also saw the rise of Ferry as a force in the Porsche organization in his own right. Ferry comes across as introvert, shy and shunning publicity, but nevertheless a man of strong will. He was *not* going to sit back and bask in his father's glory: he would make his own way in life. Having the Professor as a father was in many ways an advantage, since he could absorb automotive design almost by osmosis — yet it could also be a drawback. For example, there were those who did not or would not believe he was a real engineer: he had to prove otherwise.

His methods were almost the total opposite of his father's. Porsche senior was an intuitive engineer, relying on flair and genius, constantly coming up with new ideas, and almost losing interest in problems once they had been solved. Ferry believed much more in the steady, unspectacular refinement and solid development of an idea to the point where it was more than just feasible or even satisfactory: it had to be correct from all viewpoints.

It is in fact Ferry's philosophy of 'one step at a time to perfection' that has permeated and formed the solid backbone of the Porsche company as we know it today. By following this logical step it is easy to see if the change is for the better or worse. Too many changes at once can cloud the potential issues.

Two prewar Porsche projects are worth mentioning at this point. The first was the Type 114. This was to have been a sports-racer, incorporating some astonishing ideas — such as a ten-cylinder engine! This didn't get off the drawing board, but a racing variant of the VW, designated the Type 60K10 and destined for a race that never took place (from Rome to Berlin) did see light of day. If any car could be called the true predecessor of the Porsche, it must be the Type 60K10, for it was based on VW mechanicals suitably modi-

fied with an ultra-sleek coupe body. One look at that car and its layout today and it is obvious whence came the seeds for the 356.

As the war dragged on towards its inevitable — to the Porsches, anyway — conclusion, Stuttgart and its Zuffenhausen suburb came under more and more concentrated attack. The Porsche office was obviously too important to be left there, so the authorities ordered a move to a safe area — Czechoslovakia. Ferry managed to resist this, and eventually found a small sawmill in Gmünd, in Austria, and a glider school at Zell-am-See, close to his farm. By late 1944 the Professor was ill with a gall bladder complaint, and the Porsches were already wondering which of the Allies would take over where in a defeated Germany. As the war ended, the family retreated to Zell-am-See. In the end, the Americans occupied the Zuffenhausen works and Zell-am-See came under their jurisdiction as well. Gmünd fell into the British sector. Because, as German citizens, they were not allowed to hold property, Rabe was put in charge of the Porsche interests at Gmünd and Karl Kern at Stuttgart.

The years between 1945 and 1947 saw the Porsche family at their lowest ebb. Initial Allied interrogations took place at Zell-am-See and Gmünd, and passed off amicably enough.

On 30 July 1945, however, Ferry, Anton Piëch (Ferry's brother-in-law), and other members of the Porsche staff resident at Zell-am-See were arrested and imprisoned. The charges arose from the fact that two dead bodies were found in the house that the Professor used while at Wolfsburg. They were not released until 1 November, by which time they were cleared of any complicity in the murders.

Strangely enough, in spite of his much stronger connections with Wolfsburg, the Professor was not in the groups arrested in July. Instead, in August, he was taken to an old castle near Frankfurt, under 'Operation Dustbin,' an exceedingly odd name for an operation to investigate prominent people. He was not detained for long, as he was obviously so apolitical — a point which Albert Speer made voluntarily to the Allies. On his return he set about obtaining the release of his son and the others, in which he was successful.

And then real disaster struck. Early that November a Frenchman came calling. He was a representative of Marcel Paul, then Minister of Industrial Production in France. His proposal was to produce a French 'Volkswagen'!

A meeting with the French at Baden-Baden which included the Professor, Ferry, Dr Piëch and the Professor's nephew Herbert Kaes, took place on 16 November. It was inconclusive, so the family returned to Zell-am-See. Another meeting was called, and the team returned to Baden-Baden. The whole affair seemed to be pie in the sky, so the Professor decided to return to Zell-am-See again on 16 December. The night before they were due to return they were arrested.

The arrest order had been signed by Pierre Teitgen, the Minister of Justice, and there was no love lost between him and Paul, which was probably one of the reasons for the arrests. This whole period is something of a mystery, with only Ferry's account of the affair being anything like extensive. One thing is clear: the French don't come out of it with any distinction.

What appears to have happened is as follows. Elements of the French motor industry heard of Paul's plan for a French 'Volkswagen,' and quite naturally didn't care for it – there was enough competition as it was. So they applied pressure via Teitgen. In addition, Pierre Peugeot brought charges of war crimes against the Professor.

What made these charges so odd was that Peugeot and Porsche had been on amicable terms during the war when the Frenchman's factory had been producing VW parts. In

fact, on more than one occasion, Porsche had intervened to *prevent* Gestapo action at Peugeot.

One possible explanation for this about face is that Pierre Peugeot was trying to divert attention from his own wartime activities, a theory to which Ferry subscribes. Whatever the reasons, the Professor was effectively interned, along with Dr Piëch, from the end of 1945 until August 1947. He was, by then, a tired, ill old man.

Ferry, who could show conclusively that he had had no managerial tie-up with VW, had been released over a year earlier, in July 1946. During his and his father's imprisonment up to that point the only working Porsche establishment, at Gmünd, had been run by yet another of the strong-willed Porsche family, Louise Piëch, aided by Karl Rabe. Life for her must have been especially hard, with husband, father and brother in prison.

Demands in Austria just after the war for automotive designs were few and far between. But work for the Porsche company had to be found – and it was. Farm equipment was made and repaired, and soon, too, there was a thriving business in the repair of ex-army VWs – who better to effect these than the company responsible for their design?

At the end of 1946 the Porsches had a stroke of luck. Anton Piëch's secretary had married a Viennese, Karl (later Carlo) Abarth, who had gone to live in Italy. Abarth had met an ex-Porsche employee, Rudolf Hruska, who had been stranded in Italy when the war ended. A correspondence was struck up between Abarth, Hruska and Ferry Porsche, the latter offering the other two Porsche representation in Italy. They jumped at the chance – but what was on offer?

Abarth and Hruska cast about and eventually came into

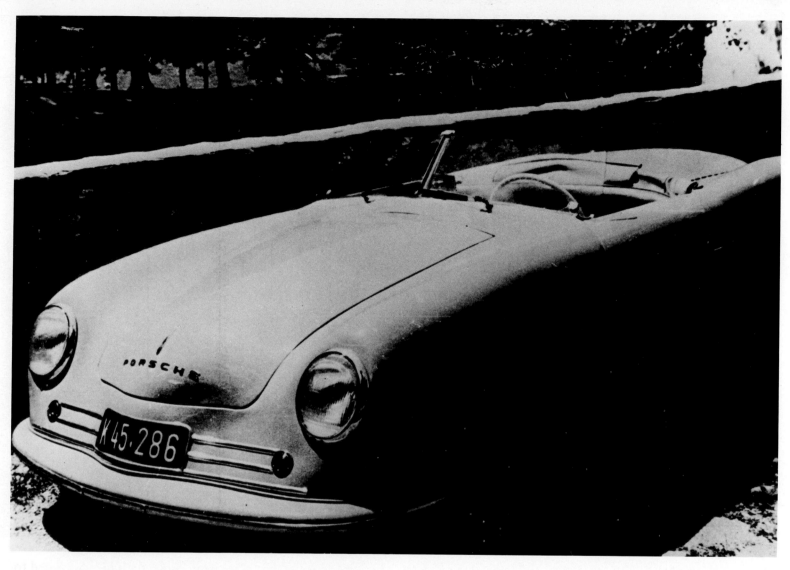

Above left: Engine assembly at Zuffenhausen in about 1950. The unmistakable figure of Dr Ferdinand Porsche is on the left, with hat: Ferry stands next to him. Above: The very first Porsche, an aluminum-bodied, mid-engined roadster. Production cars adopted the rear-engined configuration. Below: The 5000th 356 engine, a 55bhp, 1500cc unit.

contact with an Italian industrialist, Piero Dusio. He wanted a Grand Prix car: Porsche could design one. A contract was signed. Part of the contract fee, one million francs, was paid as a combination of ransom and bail for the release of the Professor.

The Grand Prix car was highly ambitious, and was to be built under Dusio's Cisitalia car company name. Cisitalia were, at the time, best known for producing little single-seat racing and two-seat sportscars, based mainly on Fiat components.

The GP car featured a 1.5-liter flat 12 supercharged engine placed (where else?) behind the driver, torsion bar suspension, and the possibility of four wheel drive. Alas only one was to be built, with parts for a few others. It was never raced, for Dusio ran into financial problems.

While the Dusio contract was on the boil, an idea that had been in Ferry's and his father's minds for a long time became firm: to build a sportscar bearing the name of Porsche. On 17 June 1947 a new project number was initiated: the Type 356.

By mid-July preliminary sketches for the Type 356 were ready. They showed a low, slippery, mid-engined roadster, using many VW mechanical parts with a space frame chassis.

In August 1947 Professor Ferdinand Porsche was released by the French. Thus he was in prison when the first of an illustrious marque was conceived.

In the last couple of years of his life Professor Ferdinand Porsche played a part in the fledgling company that rose from the ashes of the prewar concern, but such was his state of health he could really only act in an advisory capacity — which he did, no doubt, to considerable effect. However, in November 1950, he suffered a stroke from which he never recovered, and died in January 1951.

If the 1930s were the time of Ferry's effective apprenticeship for greater things, the 1940s saw him mature into a true leader, and the 1950s were to be perhaps his greatest period. Luck, reputation, contacts, all played a part in the rise of Porsche, but in those early days it was Ferry's business instinct and careful technical approach that had as much, if not more, effect. Remember, too, that Porsche were not just trying to break into motor manufacturing but were carrying on with the traditional Porsche research, design and development business as well.

Two external contracts stand out. The first arose in 1952, when the Porsche importer in America, the great entrepreneur Max Hoffman, arranged a meeting between Ferry and the management of Studebaker, the intention being that Porsche would become consultants to the South Bend, Indiana, company. An agreement was reached whereby Porsche would carry out feasibility studies on a front engined (air or water cooled, V8) car with rear wheel drive. Ferry wanted something smaller, with a rear engine naturally, but nothing came of this — until, years later, the Chevrolet Corvair appeared. However, Studebaker ran into financial difficulties, and, as with many Porsche projects, nothing was to come of their efforts.

The second contract was probably one of the most important that the Porsches ever signed. Against all predictions, VW had risen like the proverbial phoenix from the desolate remains of Hitler's one-time wonder factory. Helped at first by the British, a trickle of cars began to run off the assembly lines. And then a brilliant businessman, Heinz Nordhoff, an ex-Opel employee, took charge, and the miracle of the Beetle happened. By 1948 they were well on their way to being Germany's biggest car maker. In September of that year Porsche assumed a position they had held before the war: consultants to VW. This not only brought in an immediate cash payment, but royalties on every Beetle too. It was a financial injection that was a godsend to Porsche. In return Porsche agreed not to design a competitive car for any other manufacturer. In addition, Porsche would be responsible for VW in Austria, the Piëch side of the family looking after this business, later to become famous as Porsche-Salzburg.

All through the 1950s Porsche concentrated on one basic model, the 356, gradually developing, refining, and perfecting it in accord with Ferry's philosophy. It was a time of steadiness, growth and stability. There were but two equal partners in 'Dr. Ing. h.c. F. Porsche K.G.', Ferry and Louise.

In the late 1950s the third generation of Porsches appeared on the scene. (Ferry had four sons, Louise three and a daughter.) Ferry's eldest, Ferdinand Alexander ('Butzi') joined the company in 1957, and by 1961 was head of the styling department. His grandfather was a technical genius, his father an organizational genius; Butzi turned out to be the artistic member of the family. To him goes the credit of one of the most timeless shapes ever: the 911.

In 1961, too, another Ferdinand, this time a Piëch and Louise's eldest son, joined the company. If anything he was very much in his grandfather's mould, displaying a remarkable engineering aptitude. He swiftly took in hand the flat 6 engine that appeared in Butzi's 911. He was also responsible for one of Porsche's other all-time greats, the 917. Peter Porsche, Butzi's younger brother, also joined in 1963, to become head of production in 1965. Finally Michael Piëch joined in 1971 — but for less than a year.

Left: Ferdinand Porsche's personal 356, his last car, an early steel-bodied one built in 1950.

Below: The first steel-bodied 356 at Reutter's Zuffenhausen works. The gentlemen in hats are, from left to right, Erwin Komenda, the engineer and designer of the 356, Ferdinand Porsche, and Karl Rabe, Porsche's chief engineer.

In fact 1971 was a traumatic year for the Porsche and Piëch families. It had gradually become clear over the preceding few years that an internal battle was going on between the two branches of the family. This was bad for both and, more importantly, the company too could suffer. On top of that, with the Porsches and Piëches filling the top slots, ambitious outsiders saw little possibility of advancement, while there was always the danger that non-family members of the company would give in to family member decisions, whether they were right or not.

The cure was stunningly drastic. Ferry called a family conference in June 1971 to discuss these matters. There was really only one answer: *no* member of either family could hold a management position without the agreement of all the others — an unlikely event.

Thus the Porsche dynasty broke up. Ferry stayed on with the titular title of Chairman of the Board of Directors. Butzi started his own studios, Porsche Design, now a well-established firm whose products include the famous matt-black watch and dark glasses. Ferdinand Piëch is head of Audi engineering, and has such masterpieces as the Quattro to his credit.

But the Porsches we see on the roads today still have a family connection. They stand for all that is best in automotive engineering, a quality instilled into the company by that greatest of geniuses, Ferdinand Porsche.

Above: Classic lines – a 1958 356A. Top: A change in 1957 was the adoption of oval tail lights which replaced the previous two circular units. The small reflector above is an owner addition.

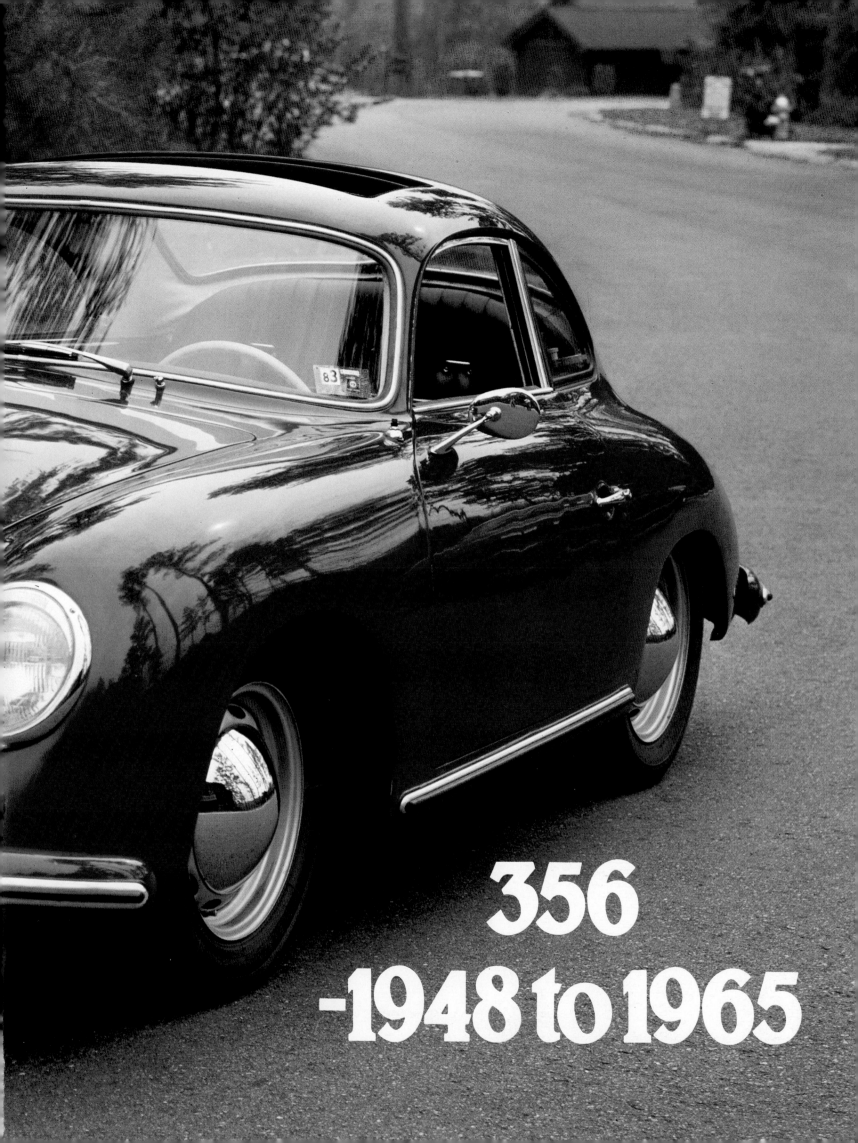

356
-1948 to 1965

By early 1948, the wooden sawmill at Gmünd saw a bodyless chassis drive off for testing: behind the wheel was Ferry Porsche. The Type 356 was rolling.

Unlike future road cars, that original 356 had a tubular space frame chassis. Another break from what was to become Porsche road car tradition was that the VW engine and transmission were reversed, with the power unit ahead of the rear axle and the transmission trailing behind. This also necessitated turning the VW rear suspension through 180°, so that the torsion bars were right in the tail. At the front standard VW suspension was fitted – twin trailing arms each side with cross tubes between them carrying the torsion bars. A mildly tuned VW 1131cc engine was used, though an increase in compression ratio from 5.8:1 to 7:1 was rather bold considering the poor quality of fuel then available.

With about 40bhp on tap, this ultra-light test chassis survived the early tests, and was then clothed with a svelte, light, open two-seater body, designed by Erwin Komenda to Ferry's specifications. The actual fabrication of the aluminum body was by a skilled panel beater, Friedrich Weber, who had the habit of disappearing every so often to imbibe a little, after which his workmanship declined: the body took a little longer than expected to make, but Weber was indispensable.

Concurrently with the open two-seater, a coupe model was being designed, the 356/2, and it was the first four of these that a Swiss, von Senger, ordered, sight unseen.

For the coupes, Ferry and Rabe reverted to the standard VW, soon to be Porsche, layout, with the engine slung behind the rear axle. There were two reasons for this. The first was that the rearward placing of the torsion tubes at the back placed stresses in the out-rigged chassis tubing that were unwelcome – one of the struts had indeed broken on trial. The second was that, with the coupe bodywork, the engine took up the space behind the seats which could be usefully used for luggage. Other reasons were that, with the engine further away, the car would be quieter, and it also meant that no fundamental change to the transmission was required for the 180 degree reversal.

Once again Komenda designed the light alloy bodywork, but this time it enveloped a sheet steel chassis, consisting of a platform with side sills and a longitudinal tunnel fronted by a boxed-scuttle-cum footwell and a fabricated section behind to take the power train and suspension. The definitive 356 basics had at last appeared.

Naturally, the engine was the VW boxer unit. Some of the first 356s were made with the standard 1131cc capacity (the first publicity brochures give this figure) but pretty soon the bore was reduced slightly, from 75mm to 73.5mm, to give a capacity of 1086cc – a figure compatible with the then-popular 1100cc class in motor racing.

That first coupe saw the light of day in August 1948, like the prototype being tested in chassis form. Gradually a trickle of cars started appearing from Gmünd – but it really was a trickle, for parts were hard to come by, and at times whatever was available would be fitted – hence, for example, the variations in engine capacity. Secondly Gmünd was way off

Top: A 1950 356 coupe, one of the first steel-bodied Reutter-built cars. Note the two-piece curved windshield and lack of quarter lights, plus flush-mounted fender.

Left: Inside the Reutter works round about 1950.

Left. One of the most charismatic and ugliest Porsches was the Speedster. This is a 1955 version. Top left. The Speedster's 1500cc engine. Top centre. With its minuscule hoodscreen, the Speedster was designed for spurs and stripping, even right down to the rear. To emphasise the humpy tail bumline Speedster was nothing of beauty, it was remarkably quick in its day.

Left: Engine accessibility was seldom a Porsche strong point. Right: For a brief period, exhausts were routed through the overriders. Far right: With no transmission tunnel to get in the way, the 356 cockpit was spacious.

Below: A late (1959) 356A coupe with sunroof.

the beaten track. Thirdly, though orders were coming in, from Holland and Portugal for example, actually obtaining permits to import Austrian-built cars into those countries was very difficult: the Dutch order was cancelled for this reason, while the Portuguese suggested an exchange of sardines for cars! Then, too, the Austrian Schilling was not regarded as hard currency, so obtaining parts from other countries including Germany was almost impossible — though von Senger helped by sending VW parts to Gmünd via Switzerland, which he could do as a Swiss national and as agent for VW in Switzerland.

The Gmünd-built coupes were quite distinctive: apart from the two-piece windscreen they had small, curved three-quarter lights in the side windows. And one of the Gmünd coupes holds a very special place in Porsche history: it was the first works entry in a major international race.

By 1949, it was obvious that Gmünd was no place to make cars: but the works in Zuffenhausen still stood, occupied by the Americans. Initial approaches for the return of the property was made through the mayor of Stuttgart, a Dr Klett. It looked as if the Porsches could have their premises back by mid to late 1950. Ferry Porsche asked an old friend, Albert Prinzing, to oversee the transfer to Germany. To keep matters ticking over there, a group of technicians was sent from Gmünd. Since there was no way they could use the works, they opened shop in the garage in the Porsche home in Feuerbacher Weg.

Obviously 'production' could not take place in such cramped conditions, even after appropriating the cook's room. In addition, rent from the Americans and royalties from VW meant that cash was accumulating, which would be highly taxable unless it was offset against a business. A restart in Germany was becoming imperative. Fortunately just down the road from the Zuffenhausen works were Reutter, the coachbuilders. Porsche took over a part of their factory to make the 356 chassis, while Reutter themselves made the bodies.

At this time, the Porsche management foresaw a maximum number of sales, world-wide, of 500 cars — how naive this seems in retrospect. However, even this number meant at least one fundamental change: the bodies would have to be made of steel, not aluminum, since the latter was in short supply and did not really lend itself to mass production at Reutters, even in such limited numbers. Komenda and the others took the opportunity to incorporate modifications too. The windscreen, for example, was lowered, widened and curved at the edges so that the distinctive Gmünd quarter lights were deleted. On Good Friday, 1950, the first German-built Porsche rolled out of Reutter's establishment.

To finance the operation, there were the VW royalties and the American's rent, but more was needed. Prinzing toured the German VW dealers and came back with firm orders for 37 cars. 500 cars world wide? By March 1951 they had made 500, and the 1000th was completed by August that year.

Those first Zuffenhausen Porsches retained many of the VW engine components, but the rest of the design was becoming more and more Porsche. There were special heads, for example, that overcame the Beetle's asthmatic breathing. With 40bhp on tap, the little low streamlined coupes could exceed 80mph quite easily, and soon private owners were entering sporting events. They were helped quite considerably at the Frankfurt Show in April 1951, where the big news was the introduction of a new engine. It had a capacity of 1300cc and produced 44bhp at 4200rpm.

That wasn't the end of the engine story that year, though. In October at the Paris Salon one of the two cars displayed, 'still liberally smeared with dead flies and dirt' as John Bolster of *Autosport* put it, was a Gmünd coupe with an even bigger 1500cc engine tucked in its tail.

It was the 1300s and 1500s that were produced in greatest quantities, and that could truly be said to have put Porsche on the map. Following Ferry's guidelines, improvements were phased in as and when they had been tested and approved, although as the historian Karl Ludvigsen says, 'in the first two and a half years at Zuffenhausen Porsche made almost as many alterations as automobiles!'

The expected return of the Porsche works in 1950 was prevented by the Korean war. A wooden prefabricated barrack block was bought in late 1950 to house the administration and design staff, but production at Reutter was severely hampered by sheer lack of space. A new factory was desperately needed: the Studebaker contract provided the necessary capital, land was bought behind the Reutter factory, and by the end of 1952 production of 356s was under way. It wasn't until 1 December 1955, that the original Porsche works were returned to the Porsches by the Americans — exactly 25 years from the date of the founding of the company.

The majority of Porsches were either coupes or the open cabriolets. In mid-1952 the bumpers were moved away from the body, and a one-piece windscreen replaced the divided one. At the same time the limitations of the VW gearbox became more and more obvious. There was the lack of synchromesh for a start: crash changes were alright for experts, but as less experienced mortals brought Porsches, so complaints increased. In addition, of course, the transaxle had been designed for puny VW outputs, not the 70bhp of the 1500. Porsche had already designed new internals, incorporating their own patented balk ring synchromesh system, for VW — and had it turned down. But the design was there: Porsche found a company, Getrag, to build the new transaxle for them. To solve some of the initial teething

Above: A beautifully maintained, English-owned 1958 356A coupe.
Below: The famous Porsche silhouette showing the exceptionally clean lines of the 356. Rounded corners, so unusual in 1958, are becoming a recognized aid to aerodynamics in the 1980s.

problems a newcomer was assigned to the job, a youngster called Helmuth Bott. The Paris Salon in 1952 thus saw the near-definitive 356.

Continuing with the main volume-produced models, the 356 design stayed relatively stable until 1955. In September 1955 a whole raft of changes were introduced. So many, that a new designation, the 356A was coined. These included an increase in capacity, from 1.5 to 1.6 liters (1582cc as against 1488cc): the suspension was modified to reduce the oversteering characteristics; and wheel diameters were made smaller (from 16in to 15in) and rim widths wider.

There were, however, a number of variations, at least a couple of which were to join the ranks of the greatest Porsches ever. The first was the Speedster.

The Speedster was really the brain-child of the ebullient Max Hoffman, Porsche's East Coast American distributor. Like the Porsches he was an Austrian by birth, and was a friend of the family. He had cashed in on the post-war sports-car boom in America via showrooms in Park Avenue in New York. Ferry thought there was a market in the States for a handful per year, but Hoffman replied that that was how many he wanted per week!

The predecessor of the Speedster came in the middle of 1952 when Porsche produced a very small run of a model called the America Roadster. These were stripped two-seaters, very light, intended mainly for racing. Their body style aft of the windscreen was unusual, too, with cutaways in the doors and humped rear fenders in place of the usual Porsche flowing line: Hoffman thought the standard Porsche 'looked funny', and this was one of Porsche's design suggestions for a more state-of-the-art shape. Considering its scarcity, the America Roadster won an inordinate number of races in the hands of such as Phil Walters, Briggs Cunningham, John Bentley, Jack McAfee and the husband and wife team of John and Josie von Neumann.

By 1954 Hoffman was pressing for a 'cheap' Porsche. The team at Zuffenhausen resurected the America Roadster design but the basis was the cabriolet, since it had the strengthening necessary for a convertible. On to this Beuttler grafted a two-seater body of quite astonishing proportions: the most common comparison was of an inverted bathtub. A minuscule windscreen cut down dramatically on frontal area, but the hood that went with it removed almost all vision except directly forward. The interior trim was pared down to the minimum. Hoffman got his 'cheap' Porsche, in September 1954.

Because it was so light, the Speedster promptly became the darling of the race track. To this day it is one of Porsche's great cult cars.

Another design that would be an all time great was named after the gruelling race that ran the length of Mexico, the Carrera Panamericana, in which Porsche had distinguished themselves. In particular a special racer, the Type 550 (of which more later) had walked away with the 1500cc class in 1954, powered by an engine which made its official public debut at Paris in October 1953.

This engine was something special. It was the brainchild of Ernst Fuhrmann who had worked on the Cisitalia project and had previously designed a special camshaft for racing. It featured no less than four camshafts, two per bank, driven by shafts and bevel gears. Apart from this unusual valve train, the engine featured twin plugs per cylinder and a roller bearing crankshaft. Its quoted output was 110bhp at 7000rpm. It was not really intended to be a road-going engine, but. . . .

Above: Raised headlights and fenders were the major innovations which were introduced with the 356B.
Right: Rear view of the 356B roadster with its effective, snug hood.

Thus one of the sensations of the Frankfurt Show in September 1955 was the Carrera — the marriage of the 356 body and most of its running gear with the four-cam engine. The Carrera, like most other Porsches, would have a long and distinguished competition career, first in 1500, then in 1600, and finally in 2000cc form, by which time it was known as the Carrera 2 and had a top speed of around the 130mph mark. In spite of a racing-orientated engine it was a tractable road car, but didn't really take kindly to low speed running. This was unfortunate for those who had bought the car for its glamor — changing the plugs, all eight of them, was a long, costly and finger nail breaking operation. The ultimate development of the 356 Carrera was a lightweight, the GTL, better known as the Abarth-Carrera.

In fact the car should perhaps be better known as the Zagato-Carrera, for it was this Italian coach-builder whose designer, Franco Scaglione, produced the drawings for the shape while Zagato produced the actual aluminum bodies. Since Zagato also provided bodies for Porsche competitors

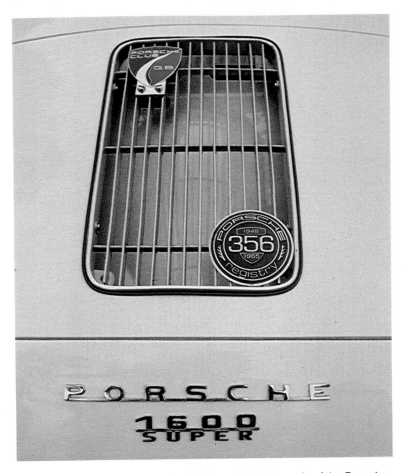

such as Alfa Romeo, it was perhaps felt politically wise for Porsche's old friend Carlo Abarth to act as front man for the tie-up: hence the name. In 1963 yet another variant of the 356 Carrera appeared, this time with a Butzi Porsche-designed body: it had a competition life of but one year, in which it was reasonably successful, and only two were built.

Reverting to the production models, 1956 saw the 10,000th Porsche roll off the lines. While 1957 saw the 1300cc engines finally dropped, diaphragm clutches first appeared – and the exhaust pipes on the pushrod engines were routed through the fender overriders. This was intended to give better ramp clearance, but merely resulted in dirtying the overriders and causing problems when the tips of the pipes rusted. Not all of Porsche's ideas were brilliant.

The Speedster was dropped too – much to the vocal chagrin of its adherents. Yet it had never been a big seller, and as it was trimmed to the bone to bring costs down, its profit margin was minimal. In 1958 it was replaced by the Speedster D (named after its body-builder Drauz), which which was more luxuriously equipped and had a 'proper' windscreen. You could even see out of it with the roof up, but the purists sneered. The name was hastily revised to the Convertible D so Speedster fanatics wouldn't be too upset.

The next few years saw steady refinement of the 356 theme, though with relatively few dramatic changes, apart from the introduction of the 356B in September 1959. The most startling was a new nose, with raised headlamps and higher, more prominent bumpers at either end. Traditionalists didn't really take to the, quite literally, facelift, but in fact it portended the shape of things to come, for there was a hint of the 911 in the lines. A new gearbox allowed the rear seats to be dropped for more headroom.

Above: Porsche badges proudly displayed – that above is of the Porsche Club Great Britain.
Below: A 1963 1.6-liter 356B Cabriolet. Below right: By the early 1960s, Porsche had forsaken the simplicity of the first cars. The interiors were plush and beautifully appointed.

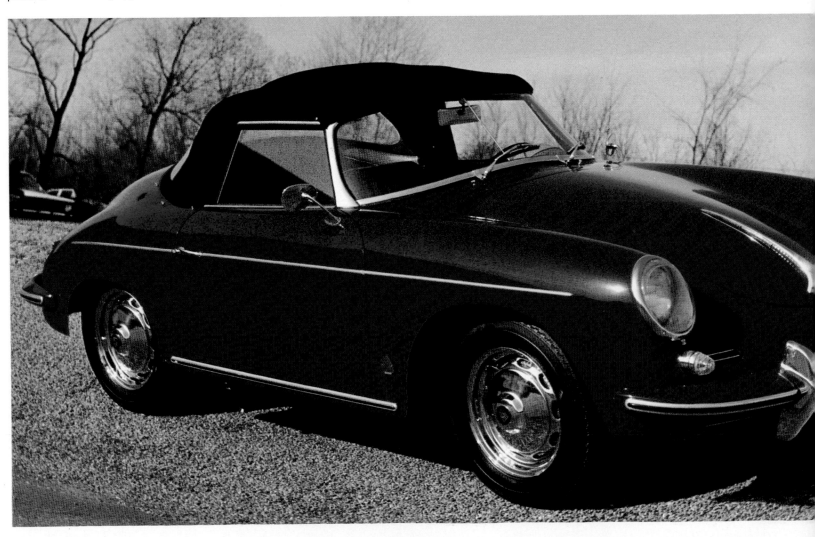

From 1958 on, only the 1600 engine was offered (Carreras apart), but in 1960 another unit was added. The cars fitted with it were called Super 90s, from the quoted output of the engine. Under the skin, too, other significant changes were incorporated in the Super 90: Koni dampers all round, and the *Ausgleichfeder*, a compensating spring, at the rear. This was a single, wide leaf spring joined to the suspension either side: it acted in the opposite sense to an anti-roll bar, thus reducing rear roll stiffness and forcing the front suspension to take a greater share of the cornering loads and hence increasing understeer. Another innovation was the adoption of radial ply tyres, but only after Porsche and Dunlop had cooperated closely to arrive at a specification that was acceptable to Porsche.

The early 1960s were the golden years of the 356 series. The range of body styles was the widest ever, with Reutter making the coupes and cabriolets, Zagato making the Abarth-Carreras, Drauz (and for a brief while D'Ieteren Frères) making the two-seater Roadsters, and Karmann the Hardtop-Coupe which, as its name suggests, was the cabriolet with a fixed roof.

Part of the reason for the diversification of suppliers was the ever-increasing production rate which was taxing the Reutter works. In 1960 the company produced 7598 cars, in 1961 7664, in 1962 some 8205, and in 1963 a total of 9672.

In 1961 another important step in Porsche history was taken: the construction of the company's new proving ground at Weissach was started. This was to grow eventually into a massive complex which could put all cars, from secret prototypes for large manufacturers to Porsche's own 917s, through their paces.

That same year saw the last of the major changes to the 356 body shell. The most obvious differences were the considerably increased glass area at front and back and twin air intakes on the rear deck. In an effort to obtain more luggage space the area under the trunk opening was completely rearranged, the gas tank being flattened and spread out, with the filler in the front wing instead of being inside the trunk.

Come 1963 the end was in sight for the 356 — from that year on the new 911 would begin to dominate. But there was still life in the old model, and in September, at the Frankfurt Show, the 356C was introduced. The major change here was the introduction of disk brakes for the first time on production Porsches. Never one to accept other people's designs if they thought they could do better, Porsche had been trying to make their own for years, but costs always worked against them. Thus it was that for the 356C Alfred Teves, under their trade name of Ate, provided the braking system — but Porsche insisted on incorporating at least one of their developments: the handbrake operated on small drums within the rear disks. With the 356C, too, the engine range was simplified even further: the 1600 standard was dropped, the 1600S or 'Super 75' as it had been briefly called became the 1600C, and the Super 90 became the 1600SC.

In 1963, too, Porsche bought out the body building side of Reutter including the factory in which they had started by renting a small corner. The part of the business they did not acquire was renamed and soon became famous as Recaro, the seat manufacturers.

After producing 16,668 of the Type 356Cs, the last of the model came off the assembly line in 1965. For a car whose originators envisaged a maximum of 500 sales, the Type 356 had become a phenomenon. When that last car rolled away, it was the 76,303rd of the model. . . .

Below: Porsche Carreras were named after the legendary Carrera Panamericana, a race down through Mexico in the 1950s. This is a 1974 911 Carrera RS. Far right: The RS's 3-liter, 230bhp flat-six engine, hidden by ancillaries.

911-Turbo power

The second generation of the Porsche dynasty and genius, in the person of Ferry, showed its ability through the Type 356. For its successor, the 911 series, the third generation proved that none of the family traditions were being diluted: on the contrary, for two of the Professor's grandchildren, Butzi Porsche and Ferdinand Piëch, were to play vital roles in its success, while Ferry still took the guiding hand as his father had done before.

By the late 1950s the 356 was an established success, and as we have ever seen, more were produced in the last few years of its life than ever before. But from an ultra-light, super-smooth, rather spartan little GT it had, over the years, put on weight, become more luxurious, required ever more powerful engines to keep up, and of course its price had put it in the realms of the upper end of the sportscar market. It had never been cheap: when first introduced into America it cost more than a Cadillac convertible or an XK120.

Quality and engineering were the 356's plus points, but over the years some of the very factors that made it so successful began to appear as drawbacks as Porsche ownership increased. The lack of space for people and luggage became a growing criticism. The handling, too, was a bone of contention: drivers either loved it or hated it. Porsche's engineers had, by constant development, managed to keep one step ahead of downright condemnation. And what had been a startling speed capability in the early years (regardless of engine size) was beginning to look, if not humdrum, then nothing particularly special, as more ordinary and cheaper cars caught up.

So it was that in 1959 Ferry Porsche gave the engineering team the go-ahead for a new type of Porsche.

By 1959 Butzi Porsche was in charge of Porsche styling, and he began exploratory work on one of the most important facets of the new car, the shape. There was one major pre-requisite: it had to *look* like a Porsche; lineality had to be maintained.

By 1962, however, there had been a fundamental change of attitude: the new car was to be a 2+2, not a full four-seater. Ferry had decided to leave such machines and their attendant bulk to the establishment: Mercedes-Benz and BMW. 'Shoemaker, stick to your last' was the way he put it. The wheelbase was brought down to a little over 4in more than that of the 356. Butzi kept the bottom half of a design that he had already evolved, adding a sleeker, slimmer roofline that retained the spirit of Komenda's 356 coupe design, but with considerably more glass area. This was the shape that was finally adopted, that was and still is one of the most beautiful and distinctive ever seen. And it *looked* like a Porsche.

While the body concept was being developed, two other areas came in for consideration. The first was the engine and transmission, the second the suspension.

Porsche's engine experience had revolved around push-rod fours, four overhead cam fours (in the Carrera), and four overhead cam eights (in racing). A lot of work had gone into the four, but it was not powerful enough for the bigger, heavier new model: the eights were powerful but complex. So a compromise was reached: a six-cylinder unit. Naturally it was to be air-cooled, and naturally it was to be sited in the tail. No other configuration was seriously considered. The man in charge of engine development was Ferdinand Piëch.

In the meantime work on the chassis/substructure was in hand. Komenda at first stuck to his guns that the new

Right: At one time, it was thought that safety regulations would dictate a roll-over bar. Porsche turned this into a selling point with the Targa model (this is a 1968 911L). Below: The superb instrumentation of a 911E.

Below right: Almost a Porsche hallmark are the chunky forged aluminum Fuchs wheels. Bottom: Butzi Porsche's immortal shape, shown here on a 1973 911E coupe.

Left: The ultra-clean lines of the early, slim 911 E before flared arches were introduced.

Right: The startling duck's-back spoiler of a Carrera RS plus the distinctive Porsche script along the tail.

car should be a four-seater, but when Ferry asked Reutter to design the underpinnings for a 2+2 he gave in gracefully and cooperated fully. The result was a monocoque unit, not dissimilar to that of the 356, clothed in Butzi's body style.

The running gear of the new car represented yet another break with Porsche tradition. Gone were the transverse torsion bars and trailing arms at the front, and swing axles at the rear.

Space was needed up front: the 356 set up took up too much. There was an elegant solution that other manufacturers had successfully adopted: MacPherson struts, first used by Ford in the early 1950s. Instead of the usual coil spring arrangement, however, the Porsche engineers couldn't resist retaining torsion bars. They did so in a way that gave them yet more luggage space, and was neat and effective: they incorporated them into the lower wishbones.

At the rear a semi-trailing arm arrangement was used, with transverse torsion bars as the springing medium.

To complete the specification, steering was by rack and pinion, disk brakes were used at each corner, and a five-speed gearbox was situated in the standard Porsche position, ahead of the engine and axle center line.

All this, then, was the basic configuration that appeared on a car, given the type number 901, that made its sensational debut at the Frankfurt Motor Show in September 1963. It is still the quintessential configuration that survives to this day, though it is probable that no single part has remained exactly as it was on that prototype. Nevertheless the layout, body shape, the flat boxer engine and suspension have remained constant in concept if not in execution.

The 901 on show at Frankfurt in 1963 was, however, just a tempter, for production would not get under way until nearly a year later. When it did start trickling off the assembly lines one problem cropped up almost immediately — one that Porsche could not have foreseen, and one which must have annoyed Ferry Porsche in particular. Peugeot, a company whose head had played such a depressing part in the imprisonment of Professor Ferdinand, objected to the name, claiming (as, under French law, they had a perfectly

legal right to) that they had cornered the market in car designations which included three numbers with a central zero (as in 104, 302, 505 and so on). This rather ignored the fact that Bristol had been making 40-cars for years, and a Porsche 904 had been running on the race tracks, so Porsche might just have a prior claim to 90-numbers. However 901 was not fully established, so Porsche simply changed the name to 911.

Thus 1964 saw the 911 enter into production, alongside the 356 initially, but at the end of 1965 the latter was finally phased out altogether.

There were, of course, teething troubles. One in particular involved the old Porsche bug-bear, handling. When the 911 appeared it was on relatively narrow tires and the weight of the engine was higher than expected. In addition the Porsche engineers were learning about the problems that can arise when MacPherson strut suspension is in volume production, as distinct from careful assembly in laboratory conditions. They were far from alone — most manufacturers who adopt this system have found themselves baffled at some time.

The net result was that the early cars understeered quite considerably under moderate cornering loads but would flick into the dreaded oversteer if the driver lifted off at high cornering speeds. In addition straight line stability was not all it should have been, and some cars had different characteristics depending on whether or not they were turning left or right! To achieve consistency, Ing. Tomala, who had succeeded Karl Rabe as Technical Director in 1962, specified incredibly close tolerances and a complex production technique. Neither really worked, and at least one odd solution, involving lumps of iron in the corners of the front fenders which affected both weight distribution and polar moment of inertia, was tried. Suspension development was in fact almost continuous, and when Ing. Tomala left Ferdinand Piëch took over as head of development. Under his rule the defects were gradually ironed out.

One of the first changes came in early 1966, with a switch from Solex to Weber carburettors to overcome a flat spot. But the real news came in August.

Below: By 1974 the rear spoiler of the Carrera RS had grown dramatically, and been tipped with rubber edging for safety. Wheels and wheel arches were becoming wider and wider too. Bottom: The front bumper-cum-spoiler of the Carrera.

Firstly there was a S version, with power up to 160bhp, giving a top speed of 140mph as against the standard car's 130mph. To go with the added performance came ventilated disk brakes, clearly visible behind meaty five-spoke forged alloy wheels, their pattern almost becoming a hallmark of Porsches for years to come.

Secondly, a brand new bodyshell also appeared that month. It was basically a convertible but incorporated a hefty roll-over bar or hoop. Like the Carrera before it, it was named the Targa after a famous race with strong Porsche connections, the Targa Florio.

Butzi, who had designed the Targa, wanted a fully opening convertible, but impending American regulations seemed to indicate at the time that such an arrangement would not meet roll-over requirements. He also wanted special panel work for the tail, but this was ruled out on cost grounds. Most importantly, however, was the fact that when the roof is chopped off a monocoque structure it is weakened considerably, and strengthening the base structure often adds more weight than the removal of the top. The hoop solved these problems.

Having come to the conclusion that the hoop was essential, Porsche turned what might have been an unacceptable feature into a novelty with such success that other manufacturers soon followed, and the generic term 'targa top' passed into motoring language. And unlike the proliferation of bodyshells that abounded with the 356, the 911 would retain but the two, the coupe and the Targa, until 1982 and the appearance of the Cabriolet.

In 1967 Porsche decided to offer an automatic trans-

mission, and the 'Sportmatic' gearbox appeared. This was in fact more 'sport' than 'automatic,' since it consisted of a normal four-speed transmission, but with a torque converter and a clutch as well. A switch in the gear lever knob caused the clutch to disengage, thus dispensing with the clutch pedal but leaving the driver still to change gear.

The first major revisions to the range came in August 1968, with the B Series. The most important of these was the extension of the wheelbase by just over two inches. This was achieved by moving the rear wheels (and wheelarches to disguise the change) back, but leaving everything else where it was. To accommodate the new angle of the drive shafts, Löbro units incorporating Rzeppa constant velocity joints were used, and the semi-trailing arms were lengthened.

The purpose behind these changes was to try and equalize the weight distribution a little more, and thus help out in the handling department. Magnesium replaced aluminum for the crankcase and twin batteries were mounted up front, improving matters even further. For the most powerful S versions, rim widths were increased to six inches. The result hoped for was achieved — the understeer was reduced at low cornering speeds and the oversteer reduced at high speeds.

For the 1969 model year, Bosch mechanical fuel injection was adopted, another significant first for production Porsches, which helped considerably towards the reduction in emissions, something which was giving automotive engineers throughout the world headaches as the American clean-air lobbyists tightened the thumbscrews. The E version also received Boge self-leveling struts at the front in place of the usual dampers as a way of improving the quality of the ride. The objective was perhaps laudable, but the units were costly and their effect on handling was questioned. Like the Sportmatic transmission, this was one alteration that was not universally accepted. The S, too, was equipped with the

Above left: The 911 Turbo placed the 911 series among the elite of the Supercar class. Left: The Turbo's instrument cluster and neat, three-spoked steering wheel. Above: With the turbocharger installed, the 911's engine bay is very full indeed.

fuel injection system, pushing power up to 170bhp at 5500rpm.

As night follows day, the C and D series followed the B for the 1970 and 1971 model years. The significant modification was the first of the increases in engine capacity, from 1991cc to 2195cc. The reason for this was to increase bottom end torque and thus driveability, notably for the American market who put great store on low speed lugging, even in Porsches.

But the 2.2-liter engine was only a brief stepping stone to the next in the series, the E and F models, which expanded capacity to 2.4 liters (actually 2341cc) via a longer stroke. At the same time, however, the compression ratio was reduced, so that the engines would run on low-lead fuel — emissions were playing an ever dominant part at this time. As power and torque had risen quite considerably since the original 2-liter was introduced, a new transmission appeared on the scene: this reversed the pattern of the previous box, putting fifth out on a limb instead of first, an arrangement that made town driving easier.

The first tentative steps towards the use of aerodynamics came in the form of an air dam under the nose of the 911S in 1972: the next year it was fitted to all models.

Thus the development for the 911 series was being set: a little bit here, a little bit there. A gradual increase in engine

capacity; wider wheels and tires to take advantage of rapidly moving technology in the tire industry; the idea that aerodynamic lessons learnt on the track could be applied to road cars; the increasing importance of emission control and safety regulations — all these factors were influential.

But if progress on the technical side was following a logical sequence, other matters weren't. Production in 1969 was 15,275 cars, in 1970 it was up to 16,761 cars. In 1971, however, inflation hit the industry world-wide, the Deutsche-mark-to-dollar rate worsened, and Porsche faced the indignity of a three-week strike, the first ever in their history. Sales fell to a disastrous 11,715. . . .

On top of that the Porsche/Piëch battle was coming to a climax. When Ferry, Louise and the rest of the family made that momentous decision not to allow individual members to hold elevated positions in the company, Heinz Branitski took over as financial director, Helmuth Bott was placed in charge of development, Anatole Lapine replaced Butzi Porsche, and at the top of the tree Dr Ernst Fuhrmann, who had been responsible for the original Carrera four-cam engine, became both managing and technical director. Almost as if in reaction to these changes, sales in 1972 picked up, to a total of 14,503 cars.

One of the first things to happen that must have pleased Ernst Fuhrmann was the reappearance of the name Carrera. This appelation had a special meaning in the Porsche dictionary, and the 911 Carrera was to be no exception — it would become one of the most sought-after Porsches ever.

The Carrera was first seen at Paris in October 1972. It was an homologation special, intended for Group 4 (Special GT) racing which required 500 manufactured. Selling 500 racers was *not* something the sales staff looked on with favor. Since it didn't conform to American regulations they couldn't sell it there. They crossed their fingers and hoped. They needn't have bothered — a week after the show they had sold their 500, by April 1973 the 1000th had been produced and homologated for Production GT (Group 3) by July that year, and at the end of the model year about 1600 had been built.

What did a Carrera buyer get for his money? First of all, yet another increase in capacity, to 2687cc (which meant the car could also be entered in up to 3-liter classes) bringing the power output up to 210bhp at 6300rpm. Then there were seven-inch wide wheels at the back, covered by wide, flared arches, and six-inchers at the front. The interior was de-trimmed. Heavier anti-roll bars and Bilstein gas-filled dampers were fitted all round.

And it looked *so* right. There was a deep dam under the nose, but even more astonishing was a strange growth on the rear lid — it looked like, and was promptly named, a 'duck-tail.' This served four purposes: it reduced lift quite considerably; it improved the drag coefficient; it moved the centre of air pressure back, which helped straight line stability in cross winds and high speed corners; and it helped cooling since the high pressure area was above the cooling vents. It also helped to keep the tail lights clean!

You could have a Carrera in any color so long as it was white, but there was a choice of colors, either red, green or blue, for the amazing 'Carrera' logo along the side, another of Tony Lapine's efforts.

It looked stunning, and had the performance to match. It had a top speed around the 150mph mark, reached 60mph from a standstill in 5½ seconds, and generated 0.9g lateral acceleration when cornering.

The 1974 model year saw a contraction in the 911 range. All models received the 2.7-liter engine, but in different states of tune and therefore output.

In addition to the bigger engine, the 1973/74 models, the G series, received Bosch's K-Jetronic fuel injection system, except for the Carrera which retained the mechanical layout.

The most distinctive alteration, however, was the appearance of heavier bumpers front and rear, to meet the American regulations which required them to be assaulted by a massive pendulum. Porsche perhaps expected an outcry similar to that which created the bigger bumpers on the 356B. In fact Tony Lapine and his team managed to integrate the design very successfully indeed, so much so that it made the earlier ones look positively dainty.

October 1974 saw yet another Porsche landmark, the introduction of the immortal 911 Turbo, but let us for the moment bring the story of the unblown cars up to date. In 1975 the Turbo's 3-liter die-cast aluminum block appeared in the Carrera 3. With this increase in capacity, peak power increased slightly to 230bhp, and flexibility improved to give a more tractable machine for traffic driving. Thus the Carrera 3 replaced the 911S, so simplifying the range to the Turbo, the Carrera 3 and the 2.7-liter 911. The latter virtually took over from the 911S, with an output (165bhp) roughly between that of the earlier 911 (150bhp) and the S (175bhp). With the introduction of the I and J series models in August 1975, all the 911 bodies were fully rust-proofed via the use of Thyssen galvanized steel for all panels.

1974 and 1975 were bad years for Porsche, following the Yom Kippur war and the fuel shortage, with production falling to 11,624 and 9710 respectively, so it was not too surprising when changes over the next couple of years were kept to a minimum. Thus it wasn't until the usual mid-year announcements in 1977 that the last, and to date last major, changes were made to the model range. The most important was the simplification, yet again, of the range: the Carrera 3 and 911 were replaced by the 3-liter 911SC. This model retained the Turbo luxury features such as the automatic heating control, and the Carrera 3's flared arches, but with the 911S's pressure-cast alloy wheels that first appeared in 1974. The engine was a slightly detuned Carrera unit giving 180bhp but again with more flexibility and little loss of performance. A Sport model, with front and rear spoilers, 16-inch wheels with 185 and 205/50 tires, and uprated shock absorbers appeared too. In 1980 a rise in compression ratio, to 9.8:1, gave an increase in power, to 204bhp.

And then a 'Studie' was shown at Frankfurt in 1981. To those who first saw it the immediate assumption was that it was Porsche's answer to Ferdinand Piëch's brilliant Audi Quattro, for it was a four wheel drive sportscar. But instead of using the logical choice for such a car, the 924, this one raised a few eyebrows, for it was nothing less than a four wheel drive 911 Turbo! Of course Porsche had experience with a rear-engined 4WD machine as far back as 1955, with the aborted Jeep-type Hunter. Almost as an aside, the body was unique: it was a fully open convertible.

Below: By 1976 the Carrera 3, fitted with a 3-liter engine, was available in Targa form (as here) and was altogether a more docile and habitable machine than the earlier 2.7-liter Carerras.
Right: The 200bhp flat-six Carrera 3 engine.

The significance of the machine only became obvious in March 1982, when, at the Geneva Show, the 911SC Cabriolet made its official bow. For the same reasons that a Targa Turbo was never offered, the new Cabriolet is only available with the unblown power unit, and is, if anything a fraction lighter than the Targa. Relatively few modifications have had to be made to the Targa shell to make it a full convertible, and those revolve mainly around the storage area for the roof when it is down.

More than once in its lifetime the 911 has been killed off by the pundits, yet the new model shows that, far from being at death's door, this amazing machine still had development potential in it. It is ironic that the car that Butzi wanted when the Targa was being developed should be the latest in the 911 saga. Not since 1965, with the demise of the 356, has there been a proper convertible in the Porsche range.

Before we leave the unblown 911s, there is one variant that ought to be mentioned: the 912. With the demise of the 356 in March 1965, and the up-market move of the 911, there was a need for a model to plug the gap until the 911 was established. Porsche took the 911 body and running gear, but slotted in the 356's 1600cc flat four with either a four-speed or optional five-speed transmission, to create the 912.

It was, if anything, more successful than the 911! In its first year 6440 were made against 4865 of the 911, followed by 8700 the following year. In fact when production ceased in 1969 some 30,300 912s had been made. It was replaced by the 914/6 as the bottom rung Porsche.

But the 912 story wasn't finished. It was reintroduced, for one year only, in 1975 (for the 1976 model year). It was sold only in America, at the insistence of Porsche + Audi, to act as a stop gap until the 924 arrived. The engine this time was a Porsche-developed 1971cc VW flat four, as seen in the last of the 914/4s, and produced 90bhp at 4900rpm. 2099 of these historic oddities were constructed.

But let us go from one extreme to the other, back to the year 1974. Porsche chose the Paris Salon to unveil one of the most charismatic cars they have ever made, and one which every Porscheophile who regards himself as a true enthusiast considers the ultimate road car – the 911 Turbo. It was Porsche's project number 930, and is often called that, but it is still officially the 911 Turbo. As with Carrera, it was intended to be an homologation special to meet impending new regulations for 1976.

Visually, with its deep front spoiler, large 'tea-tray' rear wing, hunky wheel arches enclosing Pirelli CN36 tires of 185 section at the front and 215 at the rear, the Turbo most resembled the racing Carrera RSR. From that car too came the aluminum block and cylinder dimensions, and thus the capacity of 2994cc. However the compression ratio was dropped to 6.5:1, but the increase in capacity, from the Carrera RS's 3 liters, helped recover some of the power lost when the engine was running at low speed and small throttle openings, before the turbocharger came 'on song.'

The turbocharger was by KKK, and K-Jetronic fuel injection was installed. To reduce the fabled turbo lag to a minimum, there was a by-pass in the inlet manifold, to keep compressor revs up to their working speed of the order of 90,000 to 100,000rpm. With the compressor free-wheeling, as it were, only minimal exhaust gases are needed to retain rotational speeds. To limit ultimate boost, a wastegate was fitted on the exhaust side. In this form the engine produced a splendid 260bhp.

Although the 911 had been steadily developed to take the increasing power outputs from, first, the 2.4- and then

Above: From 1979 to date the 'SC' badging has been used to indicate all the non-turbocharged 911s. Below: In spite of safety bumpers, flared arches and other styling alterations the 911 is beautiful even after 20 years.

the 2.7-liter engines, 260bhp obviously required even more up-rating. A stronger, four-speed transmission had been designed and installed. The big fat wheels demanded re-worked suspension, which included stronger bearings and altered settings. One byproduct was that the rear sheet metalwork had to be strengthened, and because of this a Targa version of the Turbo was never offered by the factory.

One major difference between the homologation special Carrera RS and the Turbo was that the former was a stripped machine with luxury touches as optional for road-going cars, but Fuhrmann insisted that the Turbo be as fully equipped as possible, almost to the 'cost no object' stage. It would be the flagship of the Porsche range.

Like the Carrera RS again, Porsche under-anticipated the demand that this sensational new car would create. In the 1975 model year, remembering it was only seen in public for the first time in October 1974, 274 Turbos were made. In the 1976 model year, this increased to 1184 road cars and 30 racers. The Turbo would never reach the figures of the lesser breeds, or even the 928, but it was a viable seller.

As ever, Porsche's mid-year press announcements in 1977 had something interesting to say. Apart from the introduction of the SC to replace the Carrera and the 911, the Turbo was uprated yet again. The bore and stroke were both increased to give a capacity of 3299cc, an intercooler was fitted, and the result was a nice, even power output of 300bhp. By this time, too, the Turbo had been sitting on Pirelli's P7s, giving tire widths of 205 section at the front and 225 at the back.

Left and below: The latest Targa 911 has a matt black roll-over bar, which plays down this once distintive feature.

In this, its form to date, the Turbo is capable of over 160mph, and can reach 60mph from a standstill in just over five seconds. A supercar by anybody's standards.

To drive a 911 Turbo is the experience of a lifetime. It can be mildly disappointing at first. You expect low speed temperament, poor town manners, a raucous engine — after all, isn't that what driving supercars is all about? Yet the Turbo is as docile as any family saloon (though you have to keep reminding yourself that it's wider than it looks from inside). And *that* is what separates the Turbo from other supercars. It is totally practical, yet its acceleration, roadholding, handling, braking and effortless speed are superior to almost everything else on the road. It sums up all that Porsche stand for. Perfectly.

Below: The 914 was a combined VW and Porsche effort, sold under both names: the 914/4 had a VW power unit; the 914/6 a Porsche one. The 914/6 was not a great success in its time, but is now a collector's item. This is a 1971 version. Above: If anything, the 914's engine was the most difficult of all to work on, access being via this narrow hatch.

14-Mid-engined experience

In the late 1950s and early 1960s the mid-engined configuration had ousted the conventional layout in the highest form of motor racing, Formula 1. The standards set there began to trickle down to production cars, slowly but surely. The world's press predicted that most sportscars would be made that way before long. The advantages were obvious from the track: better roadholding and handling. The disadvantages didn't become apparent until mid-engined cars actually appeared on the scene: awkward engine accessibility, a noise source close to the cockpit, poor luggage space, and in many instances, poor visibility.

But in 1966 mid-engined sportscars were all the rage. Naturally Porsche, with their racing experience, could build such a car. The loss of the 356 meant a lack of cheap Porsches: something mid-engined could replace it. Go back to first principles — use VW parts.

VW too could do with an image booster. The Beetle continued as ever, but potential replacements such as the Type 2 just hadn't caught on in the same way. There'd been the Karmann-Ghia, a plain jane in a party frock, but it didn't have a sporty image.

The solution to both problems seemed logical: a VW-Porsche. Using the mass-production abilities of the Wolfsburg company and Zuffenhausen brains, the result could be a car of considerable sales potential. It could even be made in two versions: a down market Porsche and an upmarket VW. One can see the appeal of the idea. Nordhoff and Ferry came to a formal agreement that Porsche would design a new sports car for VW — and an informal one that Porsche could use the model as a basis for a cheap Porsche as well.

The first problem to crop up was the looks of the car. To satisfy both companies, an outside consultant company, Gugelot Design, a well-known industrial design firm, were employed. They had styled a car for the chemical company Bayer, who were trying to promote a new structural material, using BMW mechanicals. It was this car that caught VW and Porsche's eyes, and Gugelot were given the job. The bodyshell was a monocoque structure, with bulkheads in front of and behind the front-mounted petrol tank, between cockpit and engine, and aft of the engine, in front of the rear trunk. With two trunks, one in the nose and the other in the tail, luggage space was commendable. The cockpit too was roomy — but only for two people.

The front suspension and steering was pure 911. At the

Right: The 914's shape may not have been the most attractive in Porsche history, but it solved many of the problems (such as rearward vision) of the mid-engined configuration. Below: The square tail held a big trunk.

rear semi-trailing arms located the wheels which were suspended on coil springs with integral shock absorbers.

There were two power units. For the VW car there was the new flat-four engine fitted to the VW 411. With a capacity of 1679cc, and Bosch electronic fuel injection, it produced 80bhp at 4900rpm. The version of the 914 so equipped was called the 914/4.

The other engine was Porsche's own flat-six, kept in a 2-liter form for this application after it had been enlarged to 2.2 liters for the 911.

And then tragedy struck. In July 1967 Heinz Nordhoff fell ill, and died in April 1968. His successor, Kurt Lotz, had only joined VW a few months before. He wasn't aware of the working relationship between Ferry Porsche and Nordhoff, particularly the verbal agreement in which Porsche could use 914 components for the 914/6. Lotz looked at the agreement which simply said that Porsche had designed a car for VW, who had complete rights to it. If Porsche wanted trimmed bodyshells from Karmann, he would have to pay the going rate — which was actually more than that for the 911. So much for a cheap Porsche.

To market the car, a new company was set up in Germany, owned 50/50 by VW and Porsche. In America Lotz wanted to sell the up-market Audi, but wondered if the VW image would drag it down. In America Porsche would give up its autonomy and combine with VW to form Porsche + Audi. The 914 would be known as the VW-Porsche, except in America where it would be a straight-forward Porsche.

At its launch in 1969 at Frankfurt, the 914/4 and 914/6 received a mixed reception. When the press got their hands on the cars, they tended to prefer the extra performance of the 914/6, not unnaturally, and in general the car's handling was judged as above average to good. But so was the basic 911's.

That the 914/6 was a Porsche can never be doubted — it

followed truly in the path of Ferry's original 356. The trouble was that there were those two letters, V and W, associated with it. Even in America, where it was pure Porsche, enthusiasts of the marque didn't take to it. Not just because of the VW connection, but because of the looks as well. Those who judged cars purely on merit found it a good car with excellent roadholding and handling, except at the ultimate limit.

By 1970 it was becoming obvious that the 914/6 just had the wrong image, cost too much, and wasn't accepted as a Porsche. An attempt to inject some life into it came in 1971, when some pre-production cars were made with 2.4-liter Porsche engines, flared wheel arches covering fat 185/79 × 15 Michelin tires, color-keyed front bumper-cum spoiler and rear bumper, and a rooftop welded in place. They were named the 916. Two weeks before they were due to go on show at Paris the project was cancelled. A total of 3360

Left: Like the 911, the cockpit of the 914 was very spacious – for people, at least. Above: Now you see them, now you don't. The headlights of the 914 were electrically raised. Top right: The clear, readable instruments of the 914. Right: A 1971 914 in one of the typical Porsche colors of the period.

Below: Like the 911, the 914/6 had Fuchs-forged aluminum wheels.

914/6s were made, sales towards the end in 1972 becoming a mere trickle.

The 914/4 continued for much longer and was much more successful, though, through to 1975 by which time it had been gradually improved and given more performance to go with its handling, first with a 1.8-liter and finally a 2-liter VW engine. At the end of its life the 914/4 was a much better and more reliable car, and in total 115,646 were produced.

The 914/6 project was killed by four things. The unworkability of the combined German VW-Porsche marketing company and internal politics. The second reason was cost. Thirdly it was regarded as too ugly. And finally, the car that should have been all things to all men finished up being not much to anyone. Until it went out of production, and promptly became a cult car, like the 356 Speedster — except that there were fewer 914/6's than Speedsters.

Right and below: The 924 was the first front-engined, water-cooled Porsche, but followed Porsche tradition in being based on a production VW – or, as in this case, Audi. This is the more powerful Turbo version.

924 and 928 -Front-engined revolution

I can well remember the launch of the 924. Everyone present had but one thought as the Germans, with Teutonic thoroughness, went through every detail of the car – was it a 'real' Porsche? How would died-in-the-wool Porscheophiles react to it?

For the car was as complete a break from tradition as any manufacturer has ever made. It wasn't rear engined, it wasn't air cooled. It's Audi/VW parentage wasn't hidden. Previous attempts at 'cheap' Porsches hadn't been all that successful, yet here was a car on which Porsche were going to, had no option but to, stake their future.

Only later did the realization come that in fact Porsche were following one of their longest traditions of all. What else had the first 356 coupe been but a lightweight machine based on VW mechanicals?

Yet there was another reason for its more humble componentry: as always, Porsche's external design and development section had been working hard and with considerable financial reward, and one of their contracts had been VW project 425, initiated by Rudolf Leiding, the man who converted VW from Beetle to Rabbit, from 1930's thinking to 1980's. He liked the idea of a 2+2 coupe, a sporty machine, more so than Audi's own 100 coupe. Project 425 was the result. However Leiding was replaced by Tony Schmücker who killed the project. Porsche took a gamble and a decision – *they* would make the car. Part of the deal involved in buying back the project would be that VW/Audi would build the car in the ex-NSU Neckarsulm factory. This killed three birds with one stone: it meant that VW/Audi didn't have to close down a redundant factory and thus find a way of sacking the workforce; it gave Porsche much needed additional production capacity; and it was quite close to Zuffenhausen and thus in Swabia, an area of traditional hard work and craftsmanship which Porsche valued highly, and close enough for Porsche to keep tabs on quality and other facets of production.

From the beginning of the project, one factor was constant: the power unit. This was to be an overhead camshaft version of the then-current Audi 100, which was destined for VW's LT van, the post-1977 Audi 100s, and eventually the AMC Gremlin.

In the Audi it was connected directly to the transaxle, for the 100 was a front wheel drive car. Unlike the smaller Rabbits, Polos, and Sciroccos which used a transverse layout, the big Audi used an in-line arrangement, with the engine ahead of the axle center line and the transmission behind. With this as the basic building block, what were the options open to the engineers?

The obvious one was front wheel drive. Then there was rear engined, rear wheel drive, with the power train arranged à *la* 914. Or rear wheel drive again, but with engine and transaxle reversed, à *la* 911. Finally there was the 'old fashioned' front engine, rear wheel drive configuration.

The first choice was out since, right from the beginning Porsche, if not necessarily VW, foresaw much more powerful versions, and the conflicts of power and front wheel drive were considered too complex. The second was ruled out on the grounds that one of the big complaints regarding the 914 was that 'there wasn't room to store a raincoat' in the passenger compartment – mid-placed engines may be fine for handling and image, but tend to be impractical. In addition, the 928 was already on the drawing boards, and a large and relatively cumbersome V8 twixt people and driven wheels was even less practical, and the 924 and 928 were to be the Porsches of the future: there had to be a strong family connection between the two. The same reason meant that the 911 layout was unviable.

This brought a number of additional advantages. Water cooling helped noise reduction, but so did separating the two major noise sources, engine and exhaust outlet. An engine at the front helped in overcoming crash protection regulations. Possibly most important of all, was that an equitable weight balance between front and rear could be attained, with consequent roadholding and handling advantages. It was strange indeed at that press launch to hear the engineers talking about the benefits of even balance when

A discreet rubber spoiler at the base of the rear window, badging, and special alloy wheels were identification points on the 924 Turbo.

they had practically perfected the road manners of the 911 with its pretty massive rearward weight bias.

So: the engine had to go in the front. Where to put the transmission though? Directly behind the engine as in normal practice would have meant a new box since the Audi box-cum-differential didn't lay itself open to such modification, though the planned system for the VW LT van, which did have a conventional drive, was a possibility.

The answer was technically elegant and ingenious. The Audi engine/transaxle was split behind the clutch, the transaxle moved aft and the engine left where it was. The two units were joined by a large diameter, backbone tube in which ran a small diameter propeller shaft. There were precedents for this set up. and Alfa Romeo adopted it too.

And one can't help reflecting that, somewhere ingrained in Porsche thinking, was that *some* of the mechanicals had to go at the back. . . .

The 1984cc engine, fitted with a Heron head (the bottom of the head is flat, the combustion chamber being formed in the piston) and Bosch K-Jetronic fuel injection, gave 125bhp in European form and 95bhp in detoxed, USA form. To say that most of the VW/Audi parts used in the suspension, steering and brakes, were straight from the parts bin is a gross over-simplification: Porsche added their own touches to ensure they came up to Porsche standards.

Clothing all these mechanical units was a distinctive new bodyshell. My own first reaction at that launch was that Tony Lapine's shape was curiously anonymous, almost bland, yet had a Porsche family feel to it. The nose, for example, with no obvious air intake, hearkened back to the rear-engined days. It was also rounded, smoothed, with large diameter curvature at a time when Giugiaro's trend-setting square edges — what Bill Mitchell of GM fame called 'the folded paper school of design' — was all the rage. It was not perhaps as timeless as the 911 which had and has weathered the years extremely well, but it wasn't going to date quickly either, and – for the technically minded – it had a (for then) excellent drag coefficient of 0.36. It was going to be an easy car to push through the air, with consequent benefits to speed in the upper ranges and fuel consumption.

I was probably still 911 orientated when I helped carry out one of the first full road tests of a 924 in Britain. Gone was that indescribable crackly beat from the tail, the sheer excitement of sling-shotting out of a curve, the exhilaration of a 911. In its place was a comfortable, spacious GT but not a car that got the adrenalin flowing from the moment you switched on the key. The engine sounded fussy and harsh at high revs, wind and road noise (especially over bumps) were obtrusive, and the gearshift, not perhaps surprisingly considering that the synchromesh had to deal with the inertia of the propeller shaft as well, graunched on snatched changes. And inside there was more than a whiff of VW cost-cutting about it. Perhaps because it was a Porsche I expected too much.

It positive points really only emerged after spending more time with one. It was deceptive in many ways. The performance, for example. In a 911, almost every cross-country trip was a semi-race. In the 924 you would cover the ground nearly as quickly but with very little drama. The roadholding was excellent, and the handling superb, being to all intents and purposes neutral and vice free. And there were a lot of more mundane factors going for it — such as the comparatively vast luggage space, easy to get at via a huge lift-up rear window instead of fighting it past seats. The excellent fuel consumption. The steering that was oh-so-correct. It wasn't a 911: it *was* a Porsche but of a new breed. And time will tell whether the zinc-coated sheet metal from which the 924 is made, and which allows Porsche to offer a 7 year anti-corrosion guarantee, really does work.

As ever, the base 924 has been gradually modified over its lifetime. Barely little more than a year after the first production cars rolled off the new Neckarsulm assembly line, in late 1975, the first important change was made: the VW/

Audi three-speed automatic transmission became available, while American market cars became more powerful.

Late 1977 saw another important change; a five-speed Porsche-designed transmission was offered as an optional extra. This particular box would last but a short time: in 1979 for the 1980 model seaon it would be replaced as standard with one in which fifth was out on a limb, unlike the 1977 box in which first was the odd one out. Fully transistorized ignition, a smaller steering wheel and 'black chrome' trim were also offered at the same time.

1979 saw major development number one for the 924, however: the addition of a turbocharger to create the 924 Turbo. In true Porsche tradition this was no bolt-on goodie but a thorough engineering job, enough to make the Turbo a new model.

Externally the 924 Turbo was instantly recognizable from the front by the row of four air vents across the nose of the hood to increase cooling air flow and a duct to one side of the hood. At the rear there was a discreet polyurethane spoiler around the bottom of the window.

Driving the 924 Turbo showed how much Porsche had improved matters over even a brief period. Not only was the Turbo a considerably quicker machine, but it was even more deceptively so, as Porsche deemed a boost pressure gauge unnecessary – and it was difficult to tell when the blower was in operation or not, since there was no sudden surge or high pitched whistle to say that the turbocharger was doing its work. And work on refinement too had paid off: only wind noise was below par, though the ride wasn't helped by the fatter tires.

The 1979 Frankfurt Show saw a famous name applied to what was alleged to be a one-off show car. The name was Carerra, and it was basically a 924 Turbo with flared wheel arches and fat tires. In June 1980, however, Porsche made it official. They announced the Carrera GT as an homologation special with a production run of 400 cars. As they said, 'It is intended to succeed the classic 1973 lightweight Carrera (the 911) as the ultimate road car with competition potential.'

Le Mans 1981 saw one of the world's worst-kept secrets appear on the track. It was powered by a turbocharged four-cylinder engine right enough, but had a four-valve head and twin overhead camshafts, giving 410bhp and 180mph timed along the Mulsanne straight. But afficianados, and in fact most of those at the track, knew it was more than

Top left: The plushly subtle interior of the 924 Turbo – note the 'turbo' logo on door sill.
Above: There are vestiges of VW/Audi in the dash – and no boost gauge which traditionally accompanies turbo installations.
Below: The extensive plumbing for the Bosch fuel injection and the turbocharging system, all but hide the engine.

just a one-off prototype. It heralded the new, all-Porsche engine.

Porsche announced the 944, as the new model was called, at the Frankfurt Show in September 1981. It looked basically like the Carrera GT. The chassis and running gear were developed versions of those of the 924. It was what was under the bonnet that caused all the fuss.

It was a slant four, true, but its heritage came from Porsche, not VW/Audi. To say that it was half of the 928's V8 is a fairly massive generalization, but that is basically what it was. It had a capacity of 2479cc, quite large for an in-line four, and such engines tend to be rough. Porsche had heeded the grumbles about the harshness and vibration of the early 924s, and went out of their way to make the 944 engine smoother. They did this by adding twin balance shafts, one down near the crankshaft, the other up near the head, running at twice engine speed. Then there were very special engine mounts. This may sound complicated, but having tried a PRV (the cooperative Peugeot-Renault-Volvo) V6, and another V6 based on three quarters of the 928 V8, for a variety of reasons including smoothness and assembly difficulties, the straight four was chosen. The 163bhp this engine produces slots it neatly between the 125bhp of the standard 924 and the 177bhp of the Turbo.

Mention has been made here of the 928. Speaking strictly chronologically, it should have been brought into the story

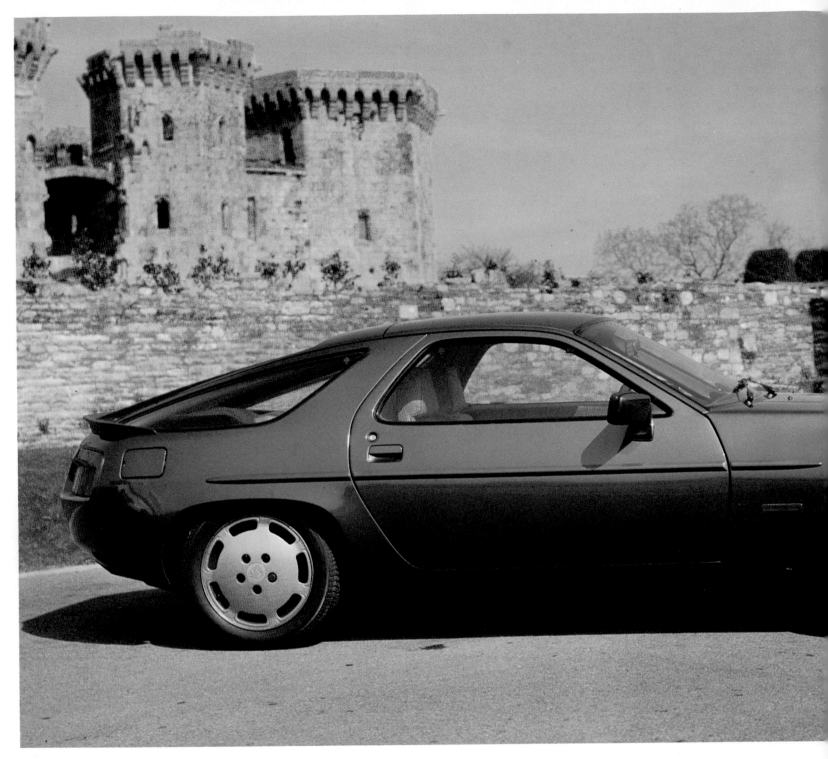

Above: Porsche's top of the range model, the 928 with the big V8 engine. The family resemblance to the 924 is obvious and in fact the 928 was on the drawing board before the 924.

at the very beginning of the chapter, since it was in the minds of the Porsche management, and on paper, before the 924 was started. But its position in the Porsche model hierarchy is such that it must be treated as a totally separate entity, and a car of equal if not greater importance.

The 928 was conceived at one of the most dramatic moments in Porsche's history. They had been working flat out on the VW EA266 project, a potential Beetle replacement with the engine tucked under the back seat. On 1 October 1971 Leiding replaced Lotz at VW — and promptly cancelled the project as he had strong ideas of his own.

The EA266 project was important to Porsche for another reason: it offered the potential for a new, small, VW-based, cheap Porsche as well. And suddenly that future disappeared.

By now, too, Dr Ernst Fuhrmann had taken over the

reins from Ferry Porsche, and one of his and his team's first decisions was to decide the future model policy. They went to the other extreme.

First, the car would have a large, relatively slow revving engine, in which refinement and smoothness would take precedence over power per liter. For years they had avoided head-on clashes with Mercedes-Benz and BMW with their coupes, but with Porsches growing ever more expensive anyway, they could see that they could take a share of the costly, luxury market. They would aim for the more mature, discerning buyer who did not necessarily want spine-tingling performance or a boy-racer image.

As with the 924, noise, emissions and safety regulations were beginning to dominate automotive design at the time too. Nobody quite knew exactly in which direction these impending laws would move — except that they would be more stringent. All the points began to indicate that the new car would have to conform to commonly accepted configurations. This meant a front mounted engine, water

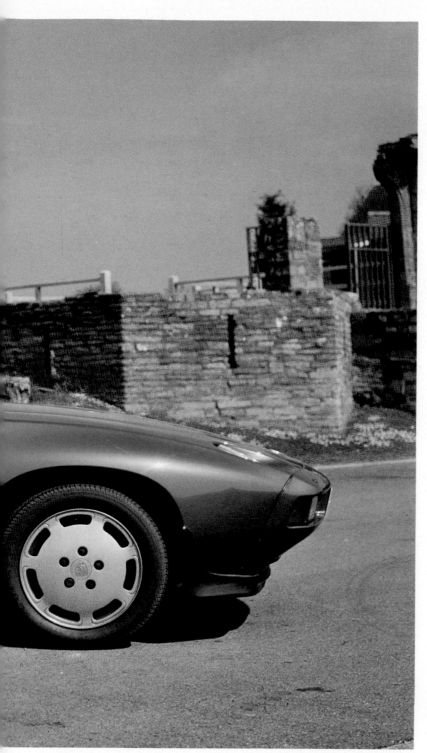

to the camshafts was via a toothed rubber belt. With Bosch K-Jetronic fuel injection it produced 240bhp at 5250rpm.

Like the 924, and again for weight balance reasons, the transmission was at the back, but, unlike the smaller car, the gearbox was ahead of the final drive, between the back seats. Five speed manual or Daimler-Benz's three speed auto boxes were the alternatives.

The suspension at front and rear also broke with Porsche tradition. There were twin wishbones, coil springs and telescopic dampers at the front, and a unique system at the back. Tires were Pirelli P7s, braking by ventilated disks all round, and steering by power assisted rack and pinion.

Naturally the shape of the monocoque bodyshell had to reflect Porsche thinking. Tony Lapine and his team set to work. Like the 924, the bumper was the most prominent feature of the nose, with intakes tucked underneath. Like the 924, too, the shape was all large diameter curves, with not a sharp edge in sight. Unlike the 924, though, the rear window didn't wrap around. Curved, narrow, triangular three-quarter windows appeared at the side, their front edges following the sharp forward rake of the door windows and B pillars. And at first sight the car didn't appear to have any bumpers at all: in fact they were covered in a flexible polyurethane plastic, color-coded to the car. The result at the rear was a bare, bulbous expanse with insets for the tail lights and licence plate. Another discussion point was that the headlamps were recessed in the hood, electrically operated to flip up when required, in the manner of the Lamborghini Miura. The 928 was announced at Geneva on 16 March 1977. Even with experience from the 924, it was like no other Porsche ever before. Traditionalists, brought up on 911 and looking for a super version, condemned it as being too slow — even with 4.5 liters it wasn't as quick as a 911, even an unblown one, on acceleration, and there wasn't much difference in top speed. And it was thirstier. Compared to its rivals, some said it was too sporty, by which they meant it didn't have the utter refinement of a Mercedez-Benz or a Jaguar; compared to a 911, it was too soft. And yet it was voted 'Car of the Year' in 1978, the Editor of *Autocar* called it 'the best car in the world' and it was one of Porsche's best launches ever.

But it was aimed at a different market to the 911. Nevertheless Porsche counteracted the lack of performance criticisms — or more likely, given the time scale, anticipated them — by introducing the 928S in August 1979. The linerless bore of the alloy engine was opened up by 2mm to give a modest increase in capacity to 4664cc. A more sporting camshaft also helped, and power rose from 240bhp to 300bhp at 5900rpm. The S could be identified from the outside by discreet spoilers front and rear, a rubbing strake down the side, and smoother wheels with peripheral slots instead of the standard cars' oval holes.

The changes may not sound like much, but they were enough to swing press opinion much more solidly behind the car: performance rose to 150+ mph, and acceleration to 60mph to the mid-six second bracket. Performance was back while consumption was, if anything, marginally better. With the 928S, and given time for the press and public alike to accept the 928 model range, Porscheophiles could relax. There *was* a 'real' Porsche at the top of the range, after all. More sybaritic, more undramatic, more refined — but a real Porsche.

Which seems as good a point as any on which to end the story of the production Porsches. With Porsches' ability to produce changes at the drop of a hat, though, by the time you read this we may be saying that about another model!

cooling, and rear wheel drive — similar constraints, as mentioned previously, would define the layout of the 924. But in the 928 and 924 Porsche would be setting the seeds for their production models for the 1980s and later, perhaps.

The decision to make the 928, and the broad concept, were thrashed out in a remarkably short time. It was to appeal to the sybaritic, but it would most definitely still be a Porsche. In fact it would also be the very first production Porsche that was all-Porsche from the ground up. The 356 had initially used VW components, the 911 carried over some 356 components. The 928 started with a blank sheet.

Initially a 3.5-liter V6 was considered, but it turned out to be too high, thanks in part to a 60 degree V angle. Eventually a 4474cc V8 was chosen.

Porsche were naturally *au fait* with state-of-the-art engineering, but the end result in the V8 was Porsche engineering at its best. All major castings were in light alloy. There were single overhead camshafts per bank, operating inclined valves in a wedge head via hydraulic tappets: drive

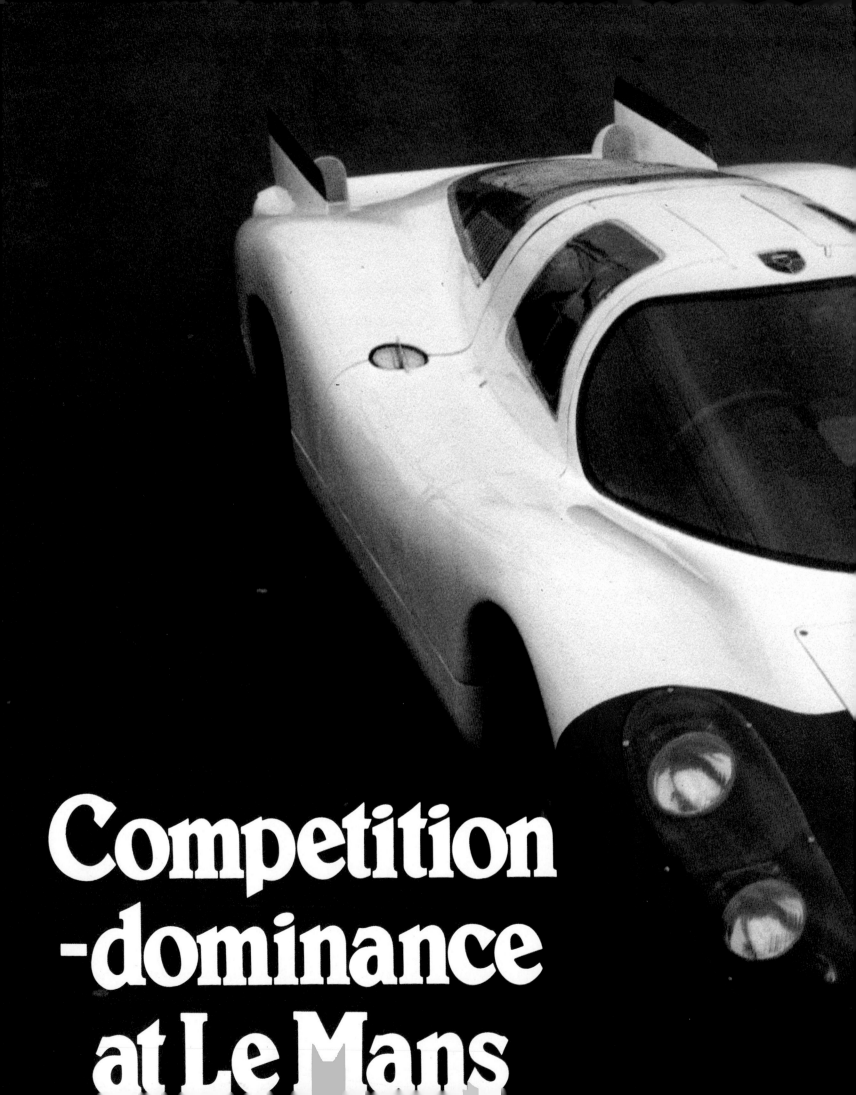

Competition -dominance at Le Mans

Above: The late 1960s saw Porsche at the forefront of aerodynamic design. Among some of the fabulous machinery they produced was this 1968 2.2-liter 275bhp 907L (L for *Langheck* or long tail).
Top: The 2-liter, four-cam, flat-four engine of the 904.

62

Porsche and competition are synonymous. Almost from the moment the first customers climbed into their little, low-slung coupes they were rarin' to go. Since 1950 barely a day, a week or a month has gone by without Porsches winning something somewhere, to such an extent that at times the company has been accused of overkill.

Porsche's sporting life can be divided roughly into four periods. There were the early days, the 1950s, with the 356-based cars. This was followed by the roadable, Carrera-engined machines. In the 1960s the mid-engined sports/racers slowly began to dominate the non-single-seater scene, culminating in the 917s. The 1970s can only be classified as the (Fuhrmann Philosophy) 911/930 era.

The first recorded win by a Porsche was on 11 July 1948, when Herbert Kaes took the very first 356, the open mid-engined car, to a class win in a round the houses race at Innsbruck. That was more of a taster than anything else, since it wasn't until 1950 that success began to be noted. Prince Joachim zu Furstenberg, co-driven by Count Konstantin Berckheim, won the 1100cc class in the Swedish Rally of the Midnight Sun, the ladies award going to Countess Cecilia Koskull in a Gmünd coupe. Later Rudolf Sauerwein and Count von der Muhle-Eckart won their class and came second overall in the Interlaken International rally — the titled and Porsches seemed to go well together! In fact both motorcars and fuel were strictly rationed commodities in those post-war years in Europe, and it was usually only the rich, the famous and the upper crust who could indulge in in such frivolity as motor sport.

With production getting under way at Stuttgart in 1950, it wasn't until 1951 that Porsches began to appear in any number on the tracks. Undoubtedly the most famous Porsche win that year was in the 1100cc class at Le Mans.

With alloy bodies and narrower roofs, the Gmünd cars were lighter and more streamlined than the Stuttgart cars, two reasons for using them in competition. For Le Mans they were further modified with louvered panels over the rear side windows, fairings beneath nose and tail, and spats over the wheel arches. The 1086cc engines had been developed to give 46bhp on the fuel available. All this was enough to give the singleton entry, driven by Veuillet and Mouche, a top speed of almost exactly 100mph, and that famous class win.

1951 also saw the introduction of both the 1300cc and roller-bearing 1500cc engines, both given a baptism of fire.

The first was in June, in an extraordinary event, the Baden-Baden rally. This called for entrants to check in at as many controls as possible in a given time. To overcome the problem of American-imposed 50mph speed limits (sound familiar?) Porsche loaned their experimental license plates to the entrants who included Prince zu Leiningen, Count Berckheim and a name that would figure prominently in Porsche history, Richard von Frankenberg, which allowed them to run flat out. The 1300s averaged 75mph for the 30 hours, with a fuel consumption of about 24mpg.

The 1500 made its bow in the infamous, car-breaking Liège—Rome—Liège rally. Two lightweight cars were entered, one an 1100cc for Huschke von Hanstein, (another name that would become famous in Porsche lore) and Petermax Muller, and the 1500, officially labelled a 1300 as the bigger unit hadn't been publicly announced, for Paul von Guilleaume and Count von der Muhle. Von Hanstein came second in class, while von Guilleaume not only won his class but was placed third overall.

The fourth significant event in 1951 was a record-breaking session at Monthléry. Three cars took part, two Gmünd coupes with an 1100 and the new 1500cc engines

respectively, and a little sports/racing open two-seater that would have special significance in later years. It was built by Walter Glöckler, a VW dealer from Frankfurt, and was naturally powered by Porsche, but with the engine reversed so that it was in front of the rear wheels with the gearbox behind.

Numerous records were taken. The 1100 coupe broke the 500 mile, 1000km and six hour records at 100.3mph, 101.4mph and 101.1mph. The Glöckler car took the same distance records for the open car class at 116.6mph, 115.3mph and 114.35mph. But most effort was concentrated on the 1500 coupe, and in spite of the loss of all gears but third, took the 72 hour record at 94.66mph. It was this car that appeared proudly on Porsche's stand at Paris a few days later.

In America, the irrepressible Max Hoffman won his class at the Mt Equinox, Vermont, hill climb on 28 October 1951 so convincingly in a cabriolet that Briggs Cunningham promptly bought one and took a first in class at Palm Springs Lake, Florida, on 8 December. Both were 1500s.

Three cars were prepared for the 1952 Le Mans race, two 1100s and a 1500: the von Hanstein/Muller car retired, the 1500 was disqualified, but an 1100, with the

Right: The 550 was the first Porsche, apart from the prototype, to be mid-engined. This is a 550A with the four-cam Fuhrmann-designed engine.

Below: Continuity – the Porsche name script has barely altered from the 1950s, as on the 550, to today.

same drivers as the year before, Veuillet and Mouche, won its class. In the Liège–Rome–Liège event Porsche almost swamped the results, with Polensky/Schluter first overall in a Gmünd coupe, a newcomer to the Porsche game called Hans Herrmann, co-driving for a Belgian, Stasse, coming in third and von Guilleaume and Scheube fourth.

The technique for cornering early Porsches had a name in German: *wischen*, or wipe. Basically the idea is similar in some respects to modern rally driving methods, in that oversteer is provoked by the driver first, the tail of the car then being controlled by the throttle and a wild sawing of the steering wheel. Get out of sequence, though, and you would execute what aviators call a 'flick-roll. . . .'.

Between 1950 and 1953, Walter Glöckler had built and raced a series of light, open, Porsche-powered specials, the first two of which were mid-engined. Glöckler was very successful with these, receiving advice and special parts from Porsche who recognized the value of his wins. Influenced by the success of the Glöckler cars, realizing that the Gmünd coupes were becoming out-dated, and that sports/racing cars such as those produced by Gordini, OSCA and others were becoming more specialized, Ferry Porsche decided in 1952 to build sports/racers.

The car was called the type 550. The basis was a simple ladder-type frame, with the usual steering, brakes and torsion bar front suspension. As the engine was placed amidships the rear suspension was turned through 180 degrees as well, with the transverse torsion bars in the rearmost cross-tube of the frame. The engine was that from the 1500 Super, but tuned to give near to 100bhp on alcohol fuel and a 12.5:1 compression ratio. The bodyshell was of light alloy and very sleek, with rather protuberant headlights and contoured fenders. Two body styles were in fact designed, one open, the other closed.

The first one to be completed ran on 31 May 1953 in the Eifel Races at the Nurburgring — and promptly won, making it a first time out winner. But this was just a trial for Le Mans.

Two cars were prepared, detuned to run on gasoline in which form they gave 78bhp. Streamlined hardtops were fitted, which deafened, cooked and gave the drivers claustrophobia, but which also increased their top speed. The driver pairings were Helm Glöckler, Walter's cousin, and Hans Herrmann making his first sortie to Le Mans, with von Frankenberg and the talented Belgian journalist Paul Frère in the second car.

The two cars circulated consistently — within a lap of each

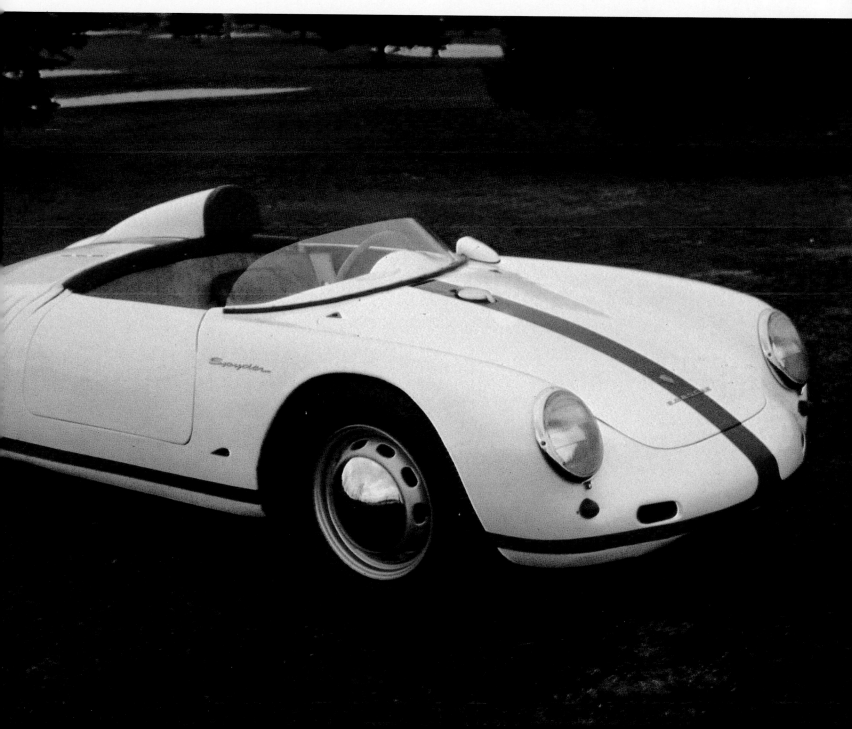

other most of the time – and fast enough to win the class with ease, the honor going to von Frankenberg and Frère.

When Ferry Porsche decided to enter the sports/racing field more seriously it was obvious that pushrod engines had their limitations, and that twin overhead camshaft units were going to be *de rigeur* for success. Egged on by von Hanstein, who was by mid-1952 both competitions manager and head of public relations, he instituted the design of a new engine. The man he and Karl Rabe chose to design the new engine was Ernst Fuhrmann. From it was to stem, in later years, a bewildering array of engines, but all with the same theme.

It was, naturally, a flat four, of 1498cc. It featured a roller bearing crankshaft and a unique valve drive train. Other features included a classic hemispherical combustion chamber and twin plugs per cylinder.

To go with the new engine, the 550 was redesigned. The chassis was modified slightly, but the most important change was to the rear suspension, the torsion bars being re-positioned in front of the axle. Komenda altered the body shape a little – not much, but enough to give the 550 a classically beautiful shape.

Two cars of the new shape were prepared for the Carrera Panamericana in 1953 in fact, and were driven by Herrmann and the 1952 overall winner (in a Mercedes-Benz), Karl Kling. Since the four-cam was not yet deemed race-worthy, they were fitted with 1500 pushrod engines, but both retired. However, Herrmann and the car he drove in 1953 took part in the Carrera again in 1954, this time fitted with a four-cam unit: he not only won his class but came in an astonishing third overall. 1954 was the last of these famous races, but the name was to live on in Porsche legend.

The first major sortie in 1954 of the four-cam 550 was the Mille Miglia on 1 May. Herrmann and Linge were entrusted with the new car, and finished a resounding sixth overall and first in class – in spite of a terrifying moment when they had to race a train to a level crossing. By ducking their heads they just made it.

Le Mans, however, remained the focal point of Porsche's efforts in 1954. Four cars were prepared for Le Mans, three with the 1.5-liter four-cam engines and one with an 1100cc version of the same. The three bigger-engined cars all suffered from holed pistons, but the Stasse/Claes 1500 carried on, and when the main competition, the OSCAs, dropped out in the last hour, staggered across the line 12th overall and the only car left in its class. The 1.1-liter car was 14th and again the sole survivor in its class.

The 1.1 car was driven by Gustave Olivier and Zora Arkus Duntov of Ardun head and Corvette fame. In discussions with Duntov about handling, Bott was told about GM's skid-pan and the results that could be obtained from it. Bott soon after found a suitable open space, at Malmsheim, and introduced skid-pan work to Porsche: again, from such humble beginnings, the vast, complex Weissach test facility would be born, and a skid-pan would play a vital part in Porsche car development.

Customer 550s started appearing in late 1954, and were officially designated 550/1500RS – until Max Hoffman, not too enamoured with numbers, suggested the model be called the 'Spyder.' From then on the name has always been used by Porsche to designate open, lightweight semi-racers or racers. In all, two 550s were sold in 1954, 63 in 1955 and 13 in 1956.

For the tragic 1955 Le Mans race, Porsche overcame the

Above: The 908's impressive 3-liter eight-cylinder engine was capable of developing some 375bhp in its day. Below: The one-piece tail of the 908/02 Spyder lifted as a whole to give good engine access.
Below left: Among other races the 1969 Spyder won the Targa Florio, taking the first four places.

piston-burning propensity of the previous year, and finished 1–2 in the 1500cc class and 1–2 in the 1100cc class as well, the leading 1.5 car placing a splendid fourth overall as well. Drivers were Polensky and von Frankenberg.

Come 1956 and the 550 received its first major revision. The early cars' frames were regarded as rather whippy, and odd things could happen to the power outputs of the engine which were traced to the fact that the distributors were driven by the camshafts.

Officially called the 550A, but more usually known as the RS, the major change was a brand new chassis, which echoed the very first type 356 in that it was a space frame. The rear suspension too was modified but in a way that broke with tradition. Gone was the simple swing axle, replaced by a low-pivot arrangement, with arms under the half shafts (which were therefore splined to accept length variations) to locate the wheels. The power output of the engine was increased. All in all, the 550A or RS was a much-modified machine: the handling was improved, thanks to the lighter but stronger chassis which overcame the ladder frame's whippiness, and the more sophisticated rear suspension, while it was faster too.

Its first appearance in April in the Mille Miglia resulted in retirement, but a month later Wolfgang von Trips and Umberto Maglioli finished fourth overall and first in class at the Nurburgring 1000kms, with Herrmann and von Frankenberg in sixth and second in class behind them.

However, 10 June 1956, saw the RS score one of Porsche's greatest wins until then, the first of a long line, in a race that, like the Carrera, would give its name to a Porsche model: the Targa Florio. Against the cream of the sports/racing cars and drivers (including Castellotti in a Monza Ferrari and Taruffi in a 300S Maserati) Umberto Maglioli drove single handed for nearly eight hours to take the chequered flag.

Development work on the 550A carried on over the winter of 1956/57, using the lessons that lightness and a smaller frontal area could be beneficial. The whole car was lowered and lightened and streamlined, with faired in headlights. The front suspension was redesigned, too. The upper tubes which carried the torsion bars were placed in a V-shape, the point being at the bottom in the middle of the frame. With the bottom tube staying as it was, the result looked like the letter K – and the new car was instantly dubbed the RSK.

However, it was given a Porsche Type number, 718, and this generic numeral would cover not just the RSKs but its good-looking and powerful successors in sportscar, Formula 2 and Formula 1 races.

The K-type front suspension was not very successful, and was dropped within the year. An RSK with this configuration practiced for the Nurburgring 1000kms in May but did not race, and its only major race that year, backing up the regular 550As, was at Le Mans where it crashed.

1957 also saw the return of Formula 2, which dictated that engines should not exceed 1.5 liters, and that ordinary gasoline had to be used. This suited Porsche well, particularly as full-width bodywork was not banned which would give the 550As and RSKs a good chance against the lighter but less powerful single-seater offerings from Britain, Lotus and Cooper in particular.

Porsche's first official entry in an F2 race was at the Nurburgring on 4 August 1957. It was run concurrently with the F1 race. Barth and Maglioli were the entries in 550As, and the former finished first of the F2 cars. A privately-owned one, driven by Porsche fanatic Carel de Beaufort, was third.

The Nurburgring 1000kms early in 1957 had seen a 550A driven by Maglioli and a newcomer to the team, Edgar Barth finish fourth and first in class. Barth had been a member of the East German EMW team, and the communists didn't take kindly to one of their comrades winning for the West Germans, especially as *they* were contesting the 1,5-liter class as well. He was informed that he wouldn't be too welcome back east, so he stayed on in the west to become one of Porsche's most notable drivers.

Towards the end of 1957 Porsche used the hill climb championship to develop enlarged versions of the four-cam engine, with capacities of 1587cc and 1679cc, so that they could compete in the 1.6 and 2-liter classes. The RSK was to spearhead the Porsche attack in 1959, so the winter months of 1957 and 1958 saw the Porsche engineers hard at work on this model, bearing in minds its F2 potential, and not ignoring the Carreras either.

In 1959 the RSK lost the K from the front suspension with a reversion to a straight tube, but not the name. At the rear a Watts linkage further located the suspension, and – at last – coil springs replaced torsion bars.

A 550A, powered by one of the 1.6-liter engines, gave the

Below: The fastest Porsche ever built, the 240mph 917/30, and above, the 956 in the hands of the most successful and popular duo to race it, on their way to victory in the 1982 Le Mans for Derek Bell's third win and Jackie Ickx's fifth.

year a rousing start in January when Moss and Behra came third in Buenos Aires. From that race on the RSK formed the backbone of the Porsche team, and it was in a 1.5 RSK that Behra, the volatile little Frenchman, came second in the Targa Florio. Initially there was some controversy over the fins – did they work or not? Some drivers liked them others didn't. At Le Mans one of the RSKs finished third overall without fins, the other fourth with them.

One of the advantages of the RSK was that the steering box was on the car's centerline, so that it could be relatively easily converted to a central driving position. Which is precisely what Porsche did for the Rheims F2 race two weeks after Le Mans. They took the Frère/Barth car which had placed fourth overall and first in the 1500cc class, adding rear wheel spats, a special tonneau cover over the cockpit and a wrap-around aero screen. Behra drove it, fins and all, and proved the point about streamlining by winning. At the Nurburgring in August a finless, spatless center-seater driven by Barth came second in the F2 section of the GP meeting, and sixth overall. But the competition from the open-wheeled cars was getting stiffer.

One other important RSK result came in October 1958 at the Los Angeles Times Grand Prix, the 'first major professional sportscar contest in post-war America.' as Karl Ludvigsen put it. Behra was placed fourth against strong, and much bigger-engined, opposition.

The FIA announced in late 1958 that, as from the 1961 season, Formula 1 would limit engine capacity to 1.5-liters, full-width bodywork would be banned, and a minimum weight limit of 1100lbs would be imposed. This gave Porsche food for thought: they had enormous experience with 1.5-liter engines, and a single-seater RSK might be competitive.

Thus the closed season between 1958 and 1959 saw the Porsche engineers and racing department concentrating on refining and obtaining more power from the RSK, and adding a single-seater program for F2, initially, but with F1 in mind, to their workload.

The F2/1 car project gathered momentum. The basis of the car was so close to the RSK that it was simply given the Type number 718/2. It used the RSK's four-cam engine and brakes, the torsion bar front suspension but the new wishbone rear, and the chassis was a simple space frame. It was covered by the bulky aluminum shell.

The works 718/2 finished third at Rheims behind Herrmann and, to gain experience with this form of racing, was entered for a minor English event, the Kentish Trophy at Brands Hatch in August. Bonnier finished third and fourth in his heats. More significantly, and perhaps the reason for bringing the car over at all, was that Stirling Moss drove it a week later in trials at Goodwood. A car was offered to Rob Walker for Moss to drive on a semi-official basis in 1960, and this was accepted by Walker.

Thus 1960 saw a works team and the Rob Walker car contesting F2, while the RSKs were updated to meet the new sportscar regulations, which called for wider cockpits, bigger windscreens, room for a 'suitcase' and spare wheel, and a production run of 100, the purpose being to make the cars more like real production machines. With blazing originality, the cars Porsche made to meet these regulations were called RS60s.

The first 718/2 went to the Walker equipe, the rest to the works team. They had a fairly eventful year: Moss was second at Brussels; Gendebien third at Pau.

For the Solitude race all five of the 718/2s produced appeared, one of them with styling by Butzi Porsche. It had a squarer, more compact, neater body with an open tail, but was not a thing of beauty. Von Trips won the Solitude race in a Ferrari, though Herrmann was second. Porsche avenged themselves at the F2 German GP in July though, finishing first (Bonnier), second (von Trips — Ferrari had not attended the meeting), fourth (Graham Hill), fifth (Herrmann) and sixth (Barth). At Zeltweg Moss, who had injured himself at Spa, returned to give Porsche a first, Bonnier followed this up with another on Ferrari's home ground at Modena, and the season came to a close with Moss winning a couple of races in South Africa.

The RS60s maintained the winning ways of the RSKs. Bonnier and Herrmann won the Targa, Gendebien/Herrman won at Sebring, and Bonnier/Gendebien were third at the Nurburgring 1000kms. But, as in 1959, there was a blot on the landscape: Le Mans. The works cars had raised rear decks and side windows to lower aerodynamic drag — almost a 'Targa' top. Only one finished, in 11th position. The other four, two works, two private, RSKs dropped out. Fortunately, as ever, customer cars kept the name of Porsche in the winners circles, all over the globe.

So successful in private hands was the RS60, in fact, that Porsche carried on making it in 1961 as the RS61.

In 1960, however, a far-reaching decision had been made: to go ahead with a new engine which, in 1.5-liter form could take on the best the F1 opposition could offer, and in 2-liter form appear in sports cars. The final configuration was an air-cooled flat-eight. However the engine wouldn't be ready for the first season of the new 1.5-liter formula, so the 718/2 was redesigned.

With a new chassis the cars were slimmer, broke yet another Porsche tradition by using twin wishbone front suspension as well (gone at last was the VW-based trailing arms and torsion bars), either four or five speed boxes, and Kugelfischer mechanical fuel injection.

The new cars were an unmitigated disaster, in spite of the efforts of Bonnier and Gurney in particular to make them competitive. After the Dutch GP at Zandvoort, when it was clear that the new 718/2s were not competitive, Ferry Porsche decided to drop them and revert to the 1960 cars — at least they were known and trusted. With them Gurney notched up three second places, at Rheims, Watkins Glen and Monza.

While offering sports RSKs to customers, and even sug-gestions and options for improvements to keep them competitive, Porsche made three specials for themselves for 1961. Two were coupes in which Butzi had taken a hand, with long, slim noses, large windscreens, and roofs that were chopped off abruptly about a foot behind the cockpit. They were called simply 718 coupes, but the third, open, car was called the W-RS.

The W-RS's first outing was to the Targa, driven by Gurney and Bonnier. It finished second behind a Ferrari, but Moss and Graham Hill had led until the last lap when a loss of oil in the transmission put them out, a few miles from the finish. This car was a 1960 RS60 but fitted, as was the W-RS, with a 1966cc plain-bearing four-cylinder engine, forerunners of those for the Carrera 2.

At the Nurburgring the W-RS was 10th after engine troubles. For Le Mans, Porsche entered all three of the new models, both coupes and the W-RS, all with different engine capacities. Masten Gregory and Bob Holbert stroked the W-RS to fifth, with Barth and Herrmann two places behind in one of the coupes.

Above and right: The 550 was not only very pretty but in its day was often capable of taking on and beating much larger engined cars.

During 1960 and 1961, the Abarth-Carreras were upholding Porsche GT honors. In 1960 one of these machines was Porsche's only official entry at Le Mans in the GT category, coming in 11th overall and first in class, while in 1961 Abarth-Carreras finished in the points in the Targa, at Le Mans, in the Paris 1000kms, and, driven by Gurney and Holbert, one came seventh overall and — of course — first in class at Sebring in early 1962.

What is there to say about Porsche's F1 efforts in 1962? Problems arose fairly quickly. The new eight cylinder engine wasn't giving quite the hoped-for outputs in 1.5-liter form. However a new chassis was designed and built for it. To some extent this followed then-current practice, with a tubular space frame, wishbone suspension at either end and a smaller, slimmer, lighter body, akin to that Butzi had produced for the F2 car, reduced frontal area.

The car's first outing, after trials at the Malmsheim skid pan had shown that it could generate the highest cornering powers a Porsche had ever achieved, was at the Dutch Grand Prix on 20 May, 1962. To show what it was up against, the same race saw the Lotus 25 in its first race — a lean, ultra-light machine, powered by the Climax V8, whose major feature broke new ground, for it was the first of Colin Chapman's monocoques. At a stroke the Porsches — and the BRMs and Ferraris *et al* — were outdated.

The F1 car's finest hour came in France, at the Rouen-les-Essarts circuit, on 8 July. Gurney, helped by an astonishing attrition rate, won. It was the car's best performance, and because other, faster machines dropped out is no cause to belittle the car's achievement. A win is a win.

A win in the non-Championship Solitude GP a week later boosted Porsche aspirations again but from then on it became obvious that it was not really competitive, and before the end of the season Ferry Porsche called a halt to F1 participation.

Why did Porsche not pursue F1? There were a number of reasons. One was that it was costing far too much money: with the other competition cars at least some of the outgoings could be recouped by selling customer versions. It was taking up a lot of the engineers' time when there were other projects, such as the potential 356 replacement, to be attended to. The engine, though a good design, obviously needed more work on it just to keep up with the opposition, never mind get ahead. There were the internal politics. But perhaps the one reason that has never been voiced publicly is that Porsche were really out of their depth in what was to them a whole new ball game, a very specialized form of motor racing. Their field was fast, rugged, reliable sportscars and long-distance racing.

This was emphasized by their other efforts in 1962 and 1963. After Le Mans in 1961 a 718 coupe and the W-RS were rebuilt and re-engined with the 2-liter versions of the eight-cylinder engine. In contrast to the F1 version, the sportscar engine seemed to suffer relatively few birth pangs.

Some ten months after Le Mans, and before the F1 car had appeared, the eight-cylindered 718 and W-RS were entered for the Targa Florio by Count Volpi's Scuderia SSS Republica de Venezia. The W-RS was in the usual Porsche silver, but the coupe was finished in the most hideous flat red. The W-RS crashed out of the race, but the red coupe struggled on brakeless to come home third.

Porsche relied again on these cars for 1963. They were rebuilt once more, this time with wishbone front suspension, and weight was cut by using glassfiber panelling, while the latest engine modifications were applied. This time the coupe driven by Bonnier and Carlo Abate pressed home to a win at record speed.

Both the coupe and W-RS retired at Le Mans, but the W-RS went on to a great and glorious career in other spheres. It was raced for a while in America, and then returned for Edgar Barth to use in the European hill climb championship, which he succeeded in winning two years in a row, 1963 and 1964. The car was entered in the 1964 Targa again, with Graham Hill and Jo Bonnier driving, but retired with half shaft trouble. So well known was this car in the Porsche competitions department that it was nicknamed *Grossmutter*, or grandmother. Edgar Barth died in 1964, and *Grossmutter* was never raced again.

904 to 917
-success
in the USA

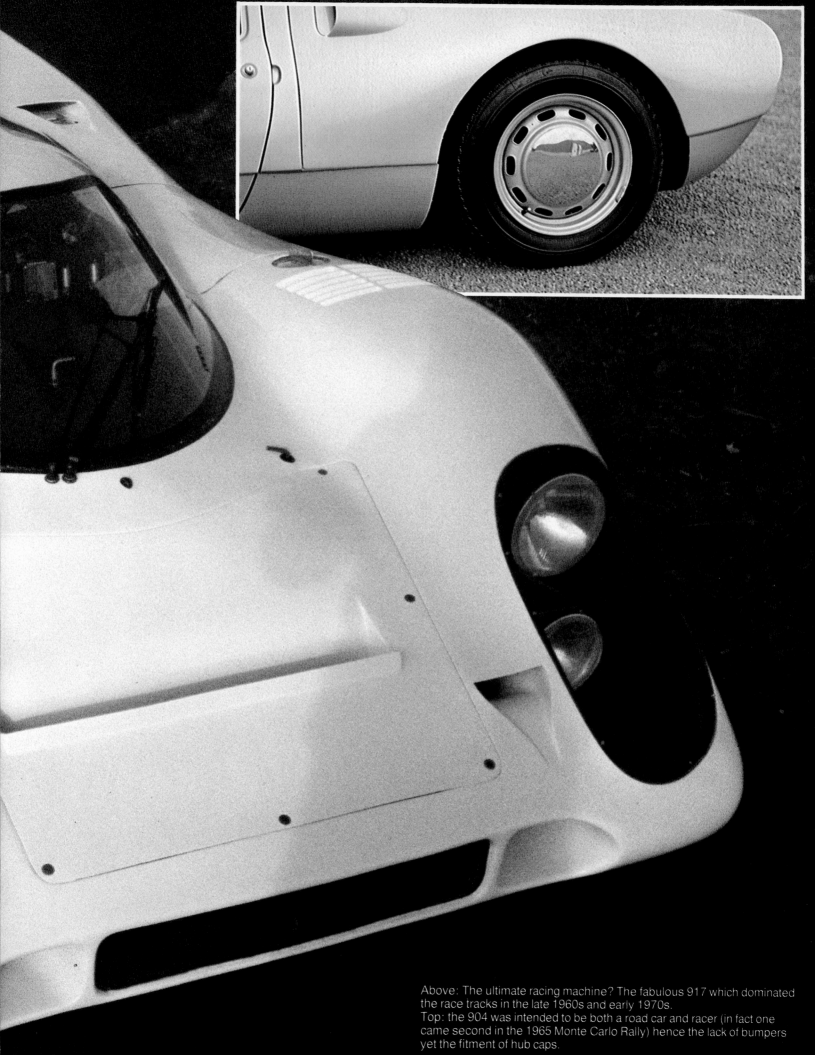

Above: The ultimate racing machine? The fabulous 917 which dominated the race tracks in the late 1960s and early 1970s.
Top: the 904 was intended to be both a road car and racer (in fact one came second in the 1965 Monte Carlo Rally) hence the lack of bumpers yet the fitment of hub caps.

The decade from 1963 to 1973 could be called the period during which Porsche grew up — or rather, during which their engines grew up. At the start the largest engine was of 2 liters, and the most powerful produced about 250bhp: by the end capacity had risen to over 5 liters, and power was a staggering 1100bhp, the most powerful racing units ever for track use. It could also be called the time of the 9-series, for it saw the 904, 906, 907, 908, 910 and 917 racers and the beginnings of the competition 911.

The early 1960s had been exhausting both in terms of cash and manpower for Porsche. There was the F1 program, initial development and design of the 911, not to mention outside contracts. And with the new 911, it was unthinkable that a Carrera equivalent could be missing from the line-up. Von Hanstein was pushing hard for something to replace the Abarth-Carreras, or GTLs as they were officially known. The RSs, RSKs and their derivatives were keeping the name of Porsche ahead on the tracks, but Porsche needed a new customer race car.

Thus the decision was taken in the winter of 1962/1963 to go ahead with a new GT model. It was called the 904.

One of the parameters laid down was that it was to use the engine and transmission from the up-coming 911 (or 901 as it was numbered internally at Porsche) but rotated 180 degrees so that the power unit was in front of the rear wheels, thus following the RS, RSK and 718 design — and cashing in on the image that such a layout could confer. It would be aimed at the 2-liter GT Championship, and therefore 100 would be made for homologation purposes.

In the end, the 911's six-cylinder engine wasn't ready in time, so the four-cylinder, four-cam engine from the Carrera 2 and Abarth-Carrera was used instead. The five-speed transmission was, however, that of the 911.

What really set the 904 apart was the body, a fiberglass affair which was bonded to the chassis for added stiffness. It was the work of Butzi Porsche, and was one of, if not the, most inspired of his works. The front section — nose and cockpit — had some affinity with the 718 coupe, but the tail curved gently around the wheels to an abrupt cut-off. Touches, such as the way the outer edge of the hood formed the inner edge of the headlamp covers, the beautiful curvature of the rear part of the roof, and the way the doors took part of the roof with them when they opened, all added up to a car that looked beautiful yet entirely purposeful.

And it was to be a production car. The standard color scheme was silver outside, blue inside, it was officially called the Carrera GTS, and the first car was delivered on 17 January 1964.

Its first race was at Sebring in March 1964. In fact five lined up, and the Lake Underwood/Briggs Cunningham car finished ninth overall and first in the 3-liter prototype class, since the homologation papers hadn't become effective.

The real sensation of the year, though, came on 26 April, when a 904, driven by Colin Davis and Antonio Pucci, won the Targa! What's more it was followed home by another 904.

The 904 had a highly successful career, including the 2-liter GT championship in 1964. Perhaps the other most historic, and certainly unusual, successes was a fighting second — in the 1965 Monte Carlo rally! It proved to be a genuine race and road car — but it was to be the last such Porsche.

The company themselves modified a few to take up the cudgels in the prototype stakes where the 718 and W-RS left off. Eight-cylinder 904s were entered for the Targa and Le Mans in 1964, but retired in both (though standard 904s

finished 7th, 8th, 10th, 11th and 12th at the Sarthe circuit that year). Through 1965 the 904 upheld Porsche colors honorably.

There was even a Spyder version, and it was this that was fitted with the engine that should have gone into the 904 in the first place — the flat six, single overhead camshaft (per bank) unit destined for the 911.

For the Spyders, the plastic bodywork was reduced to the bare minimum to cover the mechanicals, with additional strengthening to the frame to make up for any lack of stiffness. Wider and wider tires were fitted — this was the time

Top: The 904 was another of Butzi Porsche's styling exercizes — and one of his best. Above: The neat intake in the rear three-quarter panel.

Right: The 904 was intended to have the 911's six-cylinder engine but it was not ready in time, so Porsche relied on the four-cam Carrera unit.

when tire widths grew greater almost every day — the bodywork being suitably widened each time to accommodate them.

However, the 904 Spyders were significant in more than one respect. In 1965, Ferdinand Piëch took over in charge of research and development, with Helmuth Bott as his deputy. He was working his way up the Porsche ladder, and the Spyder was one step.

The 904 Spyder with box-section chassis was not a great success against Scarfiotti in the Ferrari. In the middle of 1965 Piëch and his team decided that, to make a dent in the Italian's hill-climb dominance, a brand new car was needed — in a hurry, too. The starting point was quite literally the wheels: the Ferrari was on 13 inchers, *à la* Formula 1 cars of the period, and Piëch wanted a set, and quickly. He bought them from Team Lotus at the German Grand Prix at the end of July, complete with hubs, brakes and suspension uprights. The chassis of the 904 was rejected in favor of a multi-tubular space frame, the engine was a 2-liter flat eight, and the bodywork as skimpy as possible. The car was rushed to completion and taken to Ollon-Villars in Switzerland for its debut on 29 August, barely two months after the decision to go ahead. Unfortunately it didn't win, but was from then on known as the Ollon-Villars car. This car is one of the most significant in Porsche racing history.

With the 906, the 904's replacement, Ferdinand Piëch set Porsche racing cars off on another tack. Gone was the 904 box-section chassis, replaced by a space-frame based on that of the Ollon-Villars car. The suspension was, however, more or less that of the 904, while the engine was that of the 911.

In this installation it produced some 210bhp at 8000rpm. The transaxle too was basically 911, with a load of optional transmission ratios.

The body was quite distinctive. The nose was incredibly low, with high flared wheelarches, the rear was a vast plastic window, into which were let ventilation louvers, and the tail finished off with a vestigial spoiler. The headlamp coverings were distinctive for they curved around under the bottom of the front fenders. The doors opened gull-wing fashion.

The design of the 906 had started in the fall of 1965, and if it was to meet the FIA's regulations for the 1966 Sports car category 50 would have to be made. By January 1966 all had been sold, it was announced to the public in the same month (and was given the official name of 'Carrera 6') and homologation came through on 1 May as a Group 4 sportscar.

The 906 too had its share of successes, including the almost inevitable win in the Targa Florio. For Le Mans the cars were fitted with fuel injection (which put them in the prototype category) and long tails, which in practice showed a remarkable propensity for lift-off. Small trim tabs cured this, and one of the injected cars, driven by Jo Siffert and Colin Davis, finished fourth overall behind the massive 7-liter Ford GT40 Mk 2s and won the Index of Performance, based on speed and fuel consumption.

The 906 set the pattern for the next four years, and indeed for a long time to come. A space frame, tunnel-tested aerodynamics, and a multi-cylindered engine would be seen in the next six pure racers.

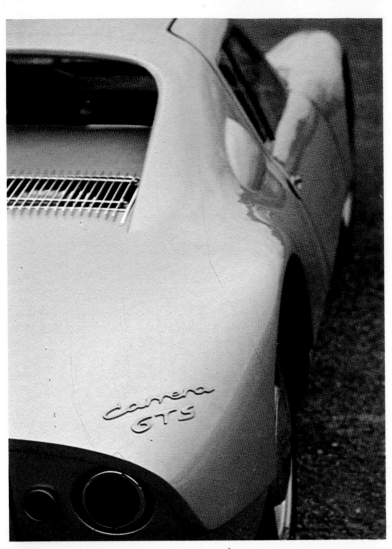

In 1966 the 911 emerged as a rally car. Vic Elford gave Porsche another of their greatest victories in 1968, by winning the Monte Carlo rally in a 911 — and the day after it finished, flew off to America for a race the next week at Daytona. He was one of the drivers that won that event in yet another new racing car, the 907. Some week! Those four years between 1966 and 1969 saw one of Porsches most hectic development periods, with new, modified, refined, or just plain different models appearing at almost every race.

First in pecking order if not in numerical sequence came the 910. This essentially took the 906's space frame, which could take either the 2-liter six or the 2.2-liter eight. From the Ollon-Villars car came the idea of the 13-inch wheels shod with fatter tires, while both the 906 and the Ollon-Villars car provided ideas for the suspension, though with new geometry and components. The body aped the 906's, but the smaller wheels meant that the front wheel arches could be reduced in size, to the benefit of forward vision. The doors too opened in the normal fashion, hinged at the front, while the large plastic rear window disappeared, and the small piece of roof between the tops of the doors could be removed if necessary to make a Spyder.

The 910 was introduced at the end of 1966 but 1967 was the year of the 910. They finished first, second and third in the Targa, filling the same three positions at the Nurburgring 1000kms and at Mugello. They were also placed in various other races. Following Porsche's usual procedure at the time, 28 910s were produced, all as works cars, but were sold off in the middle of 1967 since there was yet *another* model taking off.

This was the 907. Like the 906 and 910. it too was evolutionary, being based on the 910 chassis and running gear,

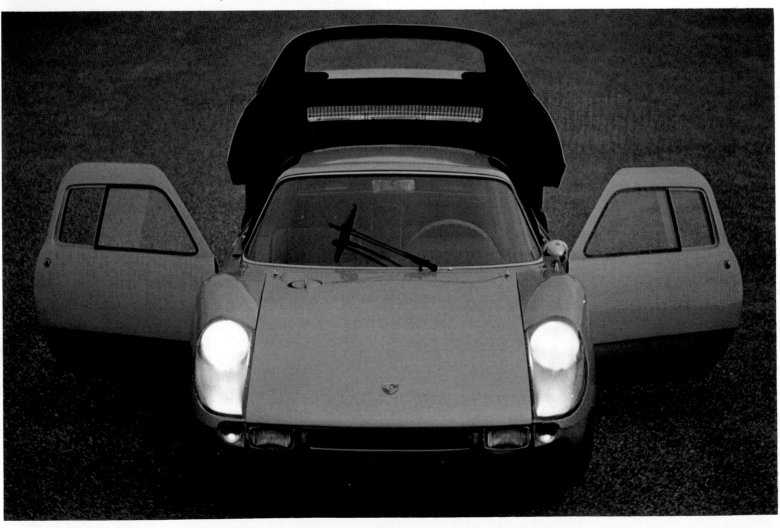

Right: As befits a high performance GT car, the cockpit of the 904 was capable of taking two in comfort even if it was rather spartan.

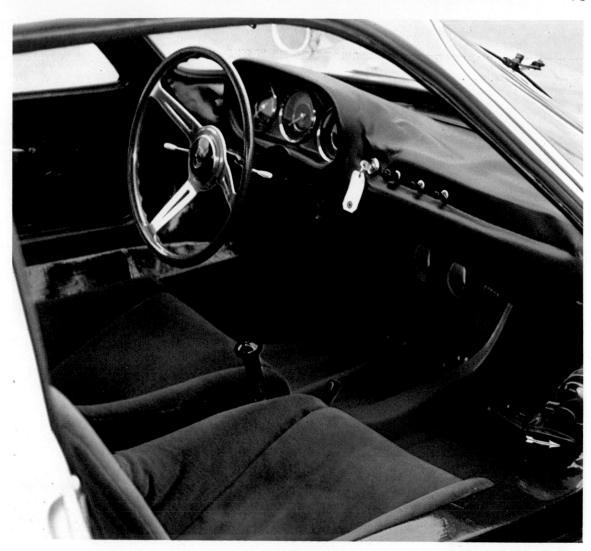

Left: The 904 was officially called the Carrera GTS. Below left: The whole of the rear opened up to reveal the engine and running gear and the doors cut into the roof for easier entry and exit.

but clothed in an astonishing new body shape. Its initial primary purpose was to win Le Mans in 1967, and for this reason the first 907s had bodies that had been finely sculptured in the Stuttgart wind tunnel. The nose was shorter and less pointed, but the tail was an incredibly long sweeping shape, curving up over the rear wheels and then back to a narrow, horizontal slit. Reducing frontal area, difficult to do with the ever-increasing width of racing tires, was achieved by making the roof much narrower: it was fronted by a vast, swept round windscreen, and backed by a long tapering rear window incorporating air ducts.

With the fiberglass of the bodies barely set, two 907Ls (L standing for *Langheck*, or long tail) were rushed to Le Mans for the practice days in April. Unfortunately the aerodynamics were far from being *au point*, and the cars were a real handful along the fast Mulsanne straight. Work around the rear end was required before the cars would be race ready.

It would be nice to report that the 907L won at Le Mans, but one retired and the other finished fifth overall, taking the Index of Performance for its speed capability and 2-liter engine.

At the press launch of the 1968 season models in December 1967, von Hanstein showed a variant of the 907L, the short-tailed 907 whose rear end owed more than a little to the hill-climb Spyder version of the 910 cars, and which was rather more practical on tighter, twisty circuits.

The 907 started its brief but illustrious career in 1968 with an amazing 1–2–3 finish at Daytona, on 3/4 February the three 907Ls crossing the line abreast, the actual winning car being driven by no less than five drivers at various times during the 24 hours. All the 907s were now fitted with the 2.2-liter four-cam engine that could trace its origins back to the abortive GP car.

23 March 1968 saw the short-tail 907s first outing — and first win, with Siffert/Herrmann coming in first and Elford/Neerpasch second. This was followed by yet another Targa win in a short-tailed car driven by Elford and Maglioli. But that was the 907's swan song, for — although it was entered in a few more races with reasonable placings — there was yet *another* model ready to pounce: the 908.

It would not be too far from the truth to say that the *raison d être* of the 908 came about because of Ford's overwhelming win at Le Mans in 1967 with the massive, 7-liter, Mk IVs. Perhaps in a fit of pique, or because they could see mega-buck companies like Ford trouncing everything in sight, the FIA announced in mid-1967 that, as from 1968, the regulations for the Sports Car Manufacturers' Championship would limit engine capacity to 3 liters for the prototypes in Group 6 and 5 liters for the Group 4 cars, of which fifty had to have been built: this was so that those people with Lolas and GT40s could still compete.

The new rules appealed to Porsche. They had the building blocks: the 907 had shown that, even in 2.2-liter form, it was highly competitive. But the ex-F1 engine couldn't be enlarged, and was in any case a complex and expensive unit. On the other hand, there was a twin overhead cam conversion available on the 901/911 engine. It could be expanded by the addition of two more cylinders. . . . .

And that was more or less what they did. Thus the 908, one of the most illustrious Porsches, was, like its predecessors, evolutionary rather than revolutionary. It was also the most powerful engine ever made by Porsche up till then, producing a conservative 310bhp when it was tested in December 1967, but this had risen to 350bhp when the car first appeared.

The 908 made its first appearance at the annual Le Mans practice days in April. Like the 907L, it was far from stable on the fast Mulsanne straight. Its first race was at Monza, where two were entered and neither finished. Two more 908Ks (K for Kurzheck, or short-tail) appeared for the Nurburgring 1000kms, and the Siffert/Elford car won.

For Le Mans, postponed that year to September, Porsche fielded four 908Ls, modified in the light of experience, with long, fixed fins over the rear wings, carrying at their extremities a fixed wing whose ends were moveable flaps, suspension-operated. By now the engines had been opened up from the initial capacity of 2921cc to 2996cc as well, and gave 350bhp. Only one survived, however, delayed by long pit stops, eventually finishing third. All in all, 1968 was not a brilliant season for the 908s.

When January 1969 came around, Porsche showed their 908 line-up, now consisting of Ls, Ks and a new model, the Spyder: as its name suggests the Spyder was the open version of the 908. They also had a new team manager, Rico Steinmann: Huschke von Hanstein was relegated once more to Press Officer.

The Spyder took advantage in a rule change for prototypes with engines up to 3 liters: they were no longer required to have a minimum ground clearance, windshield height, or room for a 'suitcase' or spare wheel. The Spyder looked like what it was — a decapitated 908K. It was called the 908/02.

Undoubtedly 1969 was the year of the 908, though it started badly when all five 908Ls retired at Daytona on the first two days of February. At Sebring, too, late in March, the best a 908 could do was a third, the car being a Spyder having its first outing.

But from then on things could hardly go wrong. Spyders took the first three places at the BOAC 500 at Brands Hatch, and then shattered the opposition in the Targa, taking the first *four* places. In the meantime a 908L had won at Monza, and another later won at Spa, in spite of the longer car's unpredictability and the drivers' dislike of it.

After the Nurburgring, in which Spyders filled the first five places, a 908L covered itself in unbelievable glory — by coming second at Le Mans. The finish that year will go down in history, for in the final hour Herrmann in the 908 and Ickx in the GT40 fought it out tooth and nail, with the younger Belgian just pipping the veteran of 13 Le Mans races. It was an epic race that can still generate considerable feeling in those who were there.

Finally, at Watkins Glen, Spyders again took the first three places — but in the last round that year another raucous bellow was heard from the tail of the winning Porsche, that of a flat 12. . . . .

The 908, no matter how brilliant, was soon to be overshadowed, and the car that was going to do it was the great 917.

When the FIA arbitrarily decreed that for the Sports Car Manufacturers' Championship prototypes would be limited to 3 liters and 'production' cars, of which fifty had to be built, could run to 5 liters, there was, not unnaturally, an outcry. Smaller companies couldn't hope to make that many: at a meeting of the CSI in March 1968 the smaller constructors put this point most strongly. In April 1968 the CSI issued another rule, which brought down the number of cars necessary to classify as 'production' to 25.

This was a number that Porsche, following their custom to sell one-race (or a-few-races-only) cars to customers, could cope with. And while the 3-liter 908s could hold their own, if Ferrari decided to go for a run of 5-liter cars they would sweep the board. And, as with the 908, and the 907

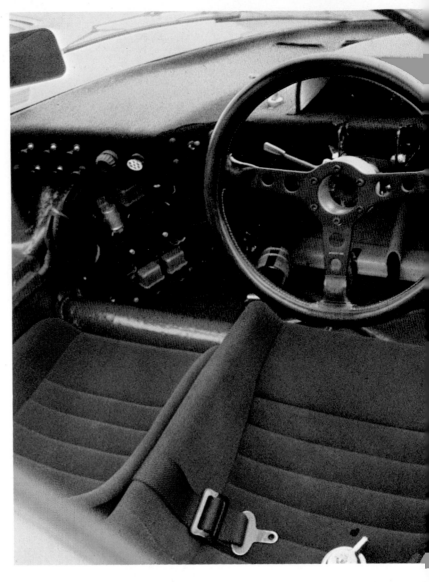

before that, and the 910, they had most of the building blocks for a new model already. In June 1968 the go-ahead was given.

Porsche often make the claim that they are in the forefront of technology. There have been times when this is so — they were among the leaders when it came to mid-engined racing cars. But on the whole their thinking is very often conservative. The 917, spectacular though it is, was not a revolutionary design.

It retained, for example, a multi-tubular space frame, admittedly made from aluminum, but by the late 1960s almost all other manufacturers were producing machines based on monocoques, as in the Ford GT40s, for example. The suspension was by conventional coil springs and wishbones — though it must be admitted again that this is still *de rigeur* wear for all forms of racing car.

The fact that time was short could well be a very good reason for this conservatism, especially if the car was to be ready for Le Mans in 1969. Thus the engine had to be air cooled: they knew about such things at Zuffenhausen. Naturally, too, it had to be a boxer.

The simple solution was to add yet another four cylinders to the 908's 3-liter flat eight. Instead of shafts and bevels to operate the valves, gears would be used, driven by one large central gear on the crankshaft dividing the engine into two six-cylinder units. One unusual feature was that the drive to the transmission was via a shaft geared to this central gearwheel as well, instead of from one end of the crankshaft. The rest of the engine — heads, valves, cylinders and so on — drew on Porsche experience. Thus there were only two

Above left: It is possible to take a passenger in a 917, but it's a tight squeeze.
Right: With the tail raised, the large opening for the air intakes and cooling fan is clearly visible.
Below: The fearsome face of a 917, in this case a 1970 4.5-liter K (short tail) model.

valves per cylinder, again at a time when four was becoming fashionable. The body shape drew strongly (for the initial cars anyway) on the 908L. Conservative, evolutionary, call it what you will, a car weighing as little as 1760lbs, with a capacity of 4494cc and 540bhp, which is what the first engines gave, would be something else indeed.

The first anyone outside Porsche (and the members of the FIA responsible for homologation) knew about the 917 was at the Geneva Motor Show which opened on 13 March 1969. Finished in plain white, with a green flash across the nose, and Shell, Dunlop and Cibie stickers on it, there was a 917 on Porsche's stand.

The FIA, realizing that a very large and powerful machine was about to drive through their loophole, wouldn't accept the partly completed cars and piles of components as proof that 25 necessary cars would be ready by 31 March at their first inspection on 20 March.

When the representatives of the CSI arrived for their second inspection on 21 April, they saw something that must have shaken them to the core: there, neatly lined up, were 25 identical white 917s!

To his regret, John Wyer's Gulf team missed out on the honors again, the Martini car of Marko and van Lennep cantering home first from the 13th hour, keeping a reasonable gap between them and the Gulf car driven by Attwood and Muller which was second.

The rules for the World Championship of makes changed for 1972, as Porsche had known all along they would. The 5-liter limit had only been given a brief life simply to give the GT40s and Lolas and the other American-engined cars an extended period of competitiveness. The fact that Porsche had seen the loophole and had reacted so quickly could not have been foreseen by any others than those at Stuttgart.

But the best was yet to come. The 917s may have been outdated in Europe and the World Championship of Makes, but over in America there was a racing series, the Can-Am, that was capturing everyone's imagination. It was for two seater sports/racers, but there was no limitation on engine capacity or a minimum weight. It was almost a case of 'anything goes.' The regular winners were Lolas and especially the Chevrolet-powered McLarens, with massive 7- and 8-liter engines. The racing was spectacular, to say the least. Could the 917s be developed in another direction?

With the creation of the Porsche + Audi operation Stateside, P+A pressed Stuttgart for a Can-Am machine to get the new set up an instant image. Porsche mounted a toe-in-the-water exercise in 1969, based on the 917 that had appeared that day at Austria when it was realized that the 917's aerodynamics were all wrong.

The 917PA was named in honor of the American company. The first one, basically just an open 917 — a Spyder in Porsche parlance — was very smooth indeed, from its low, long, slippery nose to its abbreviated tail.

Porsche had spent so much time on the 917Ls during 1969 that the 917PA was late arriving on the Can-Am scene. The driver was Jo Siffert, the man in charge Ritchie Ginther. The car was given the odd number 0!

Using a 4.5-liter engine, the car didn't do too badly, though it was fairly soon apparent that, though the aerodynamics were better than the 917 coupes, they weren't too brilliant either. It sprouted huge spoilers either side of the front wings, which were vulnerable in knock-about competition, so a new design of nose was invented, With an underpowered, barely developed car, the 917PA nevertheless gave Siffert an overall fourth in the Championship. It was promising.

Porsche backed out of Can-Am in 1970, concentrating on the manufacturers championship, but late that year the logical decision to follow the Can-Am trail, starting in 1972 when the 917's career elsewhere would be almost over, was taken.

During the winter of 1970 a new design, designated the 917/10, was put in hand. The car was based on the 917 chassis and running gear, but a new body was designed for it. Very wide to cover the fat tires, it had elements of the 917PA and 908 in its design.

To match the horsepower of the American engines, Porsche first of all enlarged the flat twelve to 5374cc, which gave about 660bhp, but at the same time started work on a much more engaging scheme: turbocharging.

By the time the Can-Am series started in 1971, Porsche were far from ready (as they knew they would be) but gave Siffert a 917/10 chassis equipped with a 5-liter engine, to make a solo foray into a series he loved. He obtained some sponsorship from Marlboro and STP but was basically paying much of the cost from his own pocket. He was showing some good placings when he was unfortunately killed in a

horrifying accident in England. That was the end of the Can-Am trail for 1971.

For 1972, Porsche wanted someone to run the team in America, along the lines of the Gulf-JW and Martini arrangement. They chose Roger Penske Racing, whose Sunoco-backed Ferrari 512 had given the 917s a run for their money at times. Porsche and Penske parried during the middle of 1971, but on 16 November it was formally announced that the two would combine to contest the 1972 Can-Am series. Their arsenal was to be the 917/10.

Penske's driver, Mark Donohue, was also a brilliant sorter of cars — and he was impressed with Porsche, and the use they made of Weissach. It was a mutual admiration society, for the Porsche engineers, from Ernst Fuhrmann, who replaced Ferdinand Piëch in October 1971 following the famous family withdrawal, on down held Donohue in the highest esteem.

Donohue stayed over in Germany, testing the 917/10, for weeks. The first car, fitted with an unblown 5-liter engine, was sent to America in December 1971 for testing on the American tracks. It proved disappointingly slow.

While Donohue spent much of the early part traveling to and from Germany, development was being carried out at Zuffenhausen on two fronts. The first was turbocharging: a 4.5-liter blown unit was sent to America in January 1972: it developed 800+bhp. But it was undriveable, the throttle acting more like an electric switch than a proper accelerator. This problem was sorted out through tinkering with the fuel

Right: This short tail body shape was only one of many used on the 917 to try and find the optimum balance between aerodynamic efficiency for high speed and stability for balance.

Below: How to transfer 580bhp to the road — massive wheels and fat Firestone tires.

injection system, which worked to Donohue's satisfaction. So the Porsche engineers promptly applied their turbochargers to a 5-liter engine, with sensational results — flash readings of 1000bhp were seen on the dynamometer!

The second front was to the running gear and body. Tests at Weissach had shown that a 100 percent locked differential gave the best handling, so the differential was deleted. A new nose was developed, whose fenders were S-shaped with a flat tray nearest the ground: between them the oil cooler was mounted in a boxy-looking structure. At the back a huge wing was supported by massive fins.

The first outing of the Penske 917/10 was at Mosport on 11 June. A little fault caused a pit stop, which slowed Donohue down and he finished second. Then, in practice for the Road Atlanta event, the rear deck came off and Donohue had a massive accident, the car destroying itself and putting Donohue in hospital. George Folmer took his place in the team, and drove splendidly — so well, in fact, that he won five races in the series to Donohue's one after his return to the track, and thus took the Can-Am Championship title for 1972.

There were other 917/10s made that year, some for Can-Am, though only the Penske team had the 5-liter blown engines all the time — the others used unblown 5.4-liter units to start with but were gradually upgraded to 4.5-liter, then 5.0-liter blown units by the end of the season. Leo Kinnunen won the Interserie championship in a 917/10.

How to begin to describe that final, last, glorious year for the 917? Penske and his team had two brand new cars to play with. They were completely redesigned, from their SERA-inspired nose, thicker and more voluptuous than that of the 917/10, to its long tail, adapted from the late 917Ls. It was longer yet slightly narrower, and the truly enormous rear wing was carried by long, long fins. With its stunning finish, in dark blue with red and yellow flashes, it looked like what it was: the most powerful racing car for road circuits the world has ever seen. The engine was a turbocharged 5.4-liter, and delivered a regular 1100bhp, though outputs up to 1500bhp and more were seen on the dynamometer.

The first two races of the 1973 Can-Am series saw other cars win, both 917/10s: an accident in the first race and a fuel leak in the second were not good omens for the 917/30. But from then on nothing could even begin to come near to Donohue: he won six of the races in the series and the Championship.

After that, both Donohue and Porsche announced retirements, the former from racing (though he did return to race in Formula 1, only to be tragically killed) and Porsche from Can-Am. The rules had been changed, so often the case when one marque is seen to dominate so completely, and the 917/30s were out of contention.

Every so often the racing world throws up truly magnificent machinery, such as the pre-War Mercedes-Benz and Auto Unions: and there is a direct line from those Auto Unions to the 917/30, the car that was the pinnacle of all that Porsche stood for.

930 Series -into the 1980s

Above: The ultimate road-going car? The Porsche 911 Turbo, here in a limited edition Martini colour scheme to celebrate a Le Mans win, must come close to that. Top left: The current 944.

1973 marks the fourth watershed year in Porsche's competition history. Life in the upper echelons of the company must have been at times exhilarating and inspiring, at times depressing and disheartening. The traumatic withdrawal of the family from an active part in the business, and the poor sales in 1971, were counterbalanced by the tremendous efforts of the fabulous 917s on the track.

When Dr Ernst Fuhrmann took over in late 1971, he must have taken a long hard look at the workings of the company, and tried to map out its future. There was at least one fairly inescapable conclusion: prestigious the 917s may have been, but the racing program was taking up too much time, effort and cost.

But his thinking went deeper than that. Did Porsche owners identify with the 917s? They were as far removed from reality as you could get. Would it not be better to develop the 911 into a machine that would not only win races and rallies, but which looked like a production car as well?

Thus this fourth period in the story of Porsche and competitons could be subtitled 'The 911 and its derivatives.'

Almost from its beginning in 1964, the 911 had been entered in competitions. Its initial successes came in rallying, with such famous drivers as Sobieslav Zasada, Vic Elford, Pauli Toivonen and Bjorn Waldegard giving them some fine victories, including three Monte Carlo rallies in a row and the European Rally Drivers' Championship in 1968 and 1970.

And, gradually too, the 911 began to appear as winners in the GT category of motor racing, at such venues as Le Mans, the Nurburgring and the Targa Florio. There was, in the 911, a firm foundation on which to build.

Fuhrmann's first step was to authorize, in May 1972, the development of a 911 variant that could begin to take on the Ferraris and other large GT cars that held sway. To do this a number of things would be required: more power, for a start; less weight for another; and improved roadholding and handling for a third.

The Carrera RS 2.7 was the result. Weight was pared to a minimum, the engine capacity was increased to 2.7 liters to compete in the 3-liter class, and wider tires under bulging wheelarches were fitted. The rules then governing the GT category allowed various modifications to be made for competition, such as even wider wheelarches and fatter tires and the extraction of yet more power. Thus was born the Carrera RSR.

The engine capacity was increased to 2806cc, which, with other modifications such as twin plug heads, gave a healthy 300bhp at 8000rpm. The oil cooler was fitted in a hole where the license plate usually goes, right in the nose. Nine-inch front and 11-inch rear wheels were standard thanks to the extra 2 inches of wheelarch width allowed, and assorted other suspension changes lowered the car and gave it tremendous roadholding.

In fact the first RSR victory came before the RS had even been homologated. It was at Daytona in February 1973, and the homologation papers for the RS didn't come into effect until 1 March. Even more astonishing was that the RSR, running as it had to in the prototype class, won overall. A battle royal developed during the race between the Penske team of Donohue and Follmer, who were to dominate the Can-Am series that year, and the Brumos Porsche car driven by Peter Gregg and Hurley Haywood, victory going eventually to the latter pair.

The 1973 works team, Martini-backed, consisted of two cars entered mainly for races counting towards the World Championship of makes. To give RSR customers a more sporting chance, one of the cars was modified way beyond what the rules allowed and thus competed in the prototype class. It won another famous international race outright, the last of the Targa Florios on the Little Madonie circuit. The other car ran in Group 4 races. Lessons learnt on the track

Below: It is a moot point which is quicker — the 911 Turbo in the foreground or the light aircraft behind. Note massive 'tea tray' rear spoiler.

were filtered through the racing services department to RSR customers.

The prototype Carrera raced by the factory had a full 3-liter (actually 2994cc) engine. This used a stronger aluminum crankcase instead of one made from magnesium.

The RSR would surely be a winner with the 3-liter engine, but how to homologate it? The answer was relatively simple: the Carrera RS had been built in such quantities (about 1600) that it qualified for Group 3, a normal production car. An evolution of the model, however, only required 100 off to be built – so Porsche built 109 Carrera RS3.0s, thus qualifying them for Group 3 for the 1974 season, with the racing version, the RSR, falling into Group 4.

The latter car had even bigger bulges around the fatter (10.5-inch front, 14-inch rear) wheels. The front fenders were widened all the way back to the leading edge of the door and there was an air duct in the front of the rear fender. The engine, in the same state of tune as the prototype from the year before, gave some 330bhp.

Three were made, and again they walked over everything in sight – and if they didn't the customer 935/76s did (a small batch had been made for sale at the end of 1976, just as a batch of 935/77s would be at the end of 1977). Once again Ickx and Mass were the major drivers, and yet again Porsche won the World Championship of Makes. By now Porsche were in an overkill situation. They so dominated those classes in which they were entered that racing began to look like a one-make affair.

For 1977 Porsche decided not to race the 936 except in one race, *the* race – Le Mans. Detailed refinements were made to the bodywork, and twin KKK turbochargers were fitted to the 2.14-liter engine. Two cars were entered, both 1976 models with the 1977 treatment. One retired, and Ickx transferred to the other which, due to a faulty injection pump, was lying way back. Slowly the remaining car worked its way up the leader board, and when the leading Renault dropped out, Ickx and Barth were in front. And then, with less than an hour to go, a piston holed. The third driver, at the wheel at the time, was Hurley Haywood: he brought the car in. Such was the lead at this point however, that the car still won in spite of having to complete the last couple of laps under its own power on five cylinders.

For 1978, Norbert Singer produced another surprise. He took advantage of the rules and removed the whole floor pan of the 935 replacing it with an aluminum tube cross-bracing frame and a fiberglass floor. This had the effect of lowering the car by no less than three inches. The nose and rear body sections were replaced by a tubular structure. With its extended nose and tail, on which sat a wing supported by triangular fins, the whole car looked decidedly weird, and was promptly nicknamed 'Moby Dick!'

In the early stages of development Singer tried the idea of

Above: The 911 Turbo's rear spoiler with intake for the intercooler. Right: The updated but still recognisably 911 interior. Below: The massive intercooler atop the engine.

joining the front and rear wings so that the sides were fully enclosed. Unfortunately the CSI wasn't going to wear this one, but eventually a compromise was reached: the front wings could extend half way back along the doors.

The most significant change, though, was to the engine. There had been growing signs that the 911-based cylinder heads were near the limit as far as performance with reliability were concerned. In addition, four valves per cylinder offered scope for yet more power.

Thus a new engine was designed. The crankshaft and crankcase remained those of the 930 Turbo, and the cylinders were still air-cooled, but new, water-cooled four valve heads were grafted on.

The new engine was laid down with three capacities: 3211cc for Group 5, 2140cc for Group 6, and 2650cc for potential use at Indianapolis. The last engine never actually appeared at Indy, since the officials insisted on a boost rating too low to give the engine a chance. The 3.2-liter capacity was chosen for the 935/78 Moby Dick car to give it maximum power and hence top speed at Le Mans. With 750bhp this was achieved, the car being immensely quick down the Mulsanne straight, but what seemed to be a serious oil leak (later found to be relatively minor) relegated it to eighth position.

Porsche's second Le Mans string for 1978 were the 936/78s. These were basically the 1977 cars but fitted with the 2.1-liter versions of the four valve water cooled head engines. Two of these were entered, along with the 1976 winner brought up to 1977 specification. One of the 2.1-liter cars crashed, the other retired, and the older car finished third. A Renault won.

In 1979, the works Porsches were limited to two of the

Above: The 944 combines the Porsche-designed 2.5-liter four-cylinder engine in the 924 Carrera's flared wheel arches and wider tires.

936s with 2.1-liter engines as of the year before. Renault had pulled out of sports car racing to concentrate on Formula 1, and the rest of the Group 6 field did not look all that strong. So at the last minute, with Essex sponsorship, Porsche entered the 936s. As expected, they dominated the early hours of the race, but the Ickx/Redman car was seriously delayed after a tire blew, and was then disqualified for receiving outside assistance. Later the Wollek/Haywood car went out with a serious misfire.

In spite of which, Porsches overwhelmed the opposition. Three 935s took first, second and third, with a 934 fourth! The winner was a Kremer-prepared car, driven by Klaus Ludwig and the Whittington brothers, with another Kremer car third, while second slot was filled by the Dick Barbour car, driven by Dick himself, Rolf Stommelen, and 54-year-old Paul Newman, the film star.

This win, along with literally hundreds of others throughout 1979, showed how much the private teams contributed to Porsches successes over the years, and how the 935s were all but unbeatable, works cars or otherwise. That year saw the 935's fourth successive win in the World Championship of Makes. Of the teams running 935s, the two that stand out are those of Kremer and Loos. The former preferred to develop their own cars, the latter relying rather more on factory advice.

In 1980, Porsche left racing to the privateers on the whole, with no works 935s, or 936s. However, the 1979 Frankfurt show had seen the return of a famous Porsche name — the 924 Carrera. Porsche made no secret that this was an homologation special and announced a production run of 400 cars. In standard form it produced 210bhp

To show the potential of this machine, a team of three were entered for Le Mans in June 1980. These were effectively out-and-out racers developing 320hp thanks to (in part) an increase inboost from 0.7 bar to 1.3 bar. As they had to run in the prototype category, almost anything went. One finished sixth, the other two 12th and 13th.

For 1981, the World Championship of Makes rules were altered, and the 3-liter limit was no longer enforced, while the IMSA American formula — basically Group 5 with detail differences — was becoming an important part of the racing scene. Thus the line-up for Le Mans saw no less than 19 Porsches out of the 55 entries — and probably the widest variety of the marque for many years. In the GTP (GT Prototype) class there was a Porsche 924 Carrera GTR, but it was no secret that the engine under the bonnet was not based on the Audi unit but on Porsche's up-coming 944. It was a 420bhp full race engine featuring twin overhead camshafts, four valves per cylinder, and a turbocharger. In Group 6 there were two more special Porsches, these being 936s fitted with the aborted 2560cc Indy engine modified to run on gasoline, but still producing some 600bhp even with low boost for long distance racing. There was also a 917, believe it or not, and Reinhold Jöst's venerable 908.

The race was a walk-over for the Ickx/Bell 936, which won by the enormous margin of 14 laps. Rondeaus filled the next two places, but a Kremer K3 935 finished fourth. The Rohrl/Barth 944 Prototype came in seventh. Neither the 917 nor the 908 lasted the distance, both being out by the seventh hour.

The company did not race any of the RSR3.0s, leaving that to their customers. And they repaid Porsche's confidence: in 1974 they won the IMSA Championship, the European GT Championship, the FIA GT Cup and a whole list of other major GT successes — then went on to repeat the same performances again in 1975.

Above left: Barely detectable differences between the 944 (shown here) and 924 cockpits.

Left: The flared wheel arches are very noticeable, the larger rear spoiler less so. Right: The 944's engine is basically half of the 928's V8 unit. Below: And still the badge stays the same. There is alleged to be a distant historic connection between the Stuttgart rampant horse emblem and another from Modena.

Porsche declared that they would enter a Turbo Carrera in Group 5 in the World Championship of Makes in 1974. This set an upper limit of three liters unblown, which reduced by a factor of 1.4 if a turbocharger was used. The cars would face a full complement of out-and-out racers such as the Matras, Alfas and Mirages. But there were also rumors that, as from 1975 or 1976, the World Championship of Makes would be for Group 5 production-based cars — something that would suit Porsche admirably.

Thus the 2.14-liter Turbo Carrera came into being. The odd capacity comes from the 1.4 equivalence factor.

The drivers during 1974 were Herbert Muller and Gijs van Lennepp, and their last result was a second place at Le Mans. They achieved the same position at Watkins Glen, were third at Spa, fifth at Monza, sixth at the Nurburgring, and seventh at Paul Ricard. These were fine results for a car that, although ultra-light and producing 450bhp (give or take a few depending on boost pressure) was still under the skin a production car.

There were no works Porsches in 1975, since the new regulations had indeed been announced for the 1976 season. They included Groups 3 (Production Touring Cars), 4 (Limited Production GT Cars), and 5, which was in fact the class for the World Championship of makes. This group (5) more or less encompassed Groups 1 to 4 but with considerable modifications allowed and a minimum weight based on a sliding scale depending on engine capacity, while the basic bodyshell, the major castings and their location, the general layout and the type of suspension had to be standard. Group 6 was for Prototypes.

Porsche attacked on three fronts — Groups 4, 5 and 6.

For Group 4, the 934 was created. The name is significant, since it indicates that it is based on the Type 930, for Group 4, the same applies for their other new models, the 935 and the 936.

The 934, with the blown 3-liter engine, had an imaginary capacity of 4.2 liters when the turbocharger equivalency rule came into play. To bring it up to the minimum weight limit it was barely stripped at all — even the electric windows were left in place! There was a reinforcing bar between the MacPherson strut suspension towers and an x-shaped cross brace above the luggage space. It was fitted with BBS 16-inch wheels.

The 934 had its share of success in the 1976 season, winning the Trans-Am Championship with George Follmer and the European GT Championship with Toine Hezemans.

Porsches second string to their bow was to become one of the most famous racing cars in the history of the sport. It was the immortal 935.

Porsche drew on their experience with the 2.14-liter Turbo Carrera of 1974. To keep below the effective 4-liter class, and therefore the weight down, a capacity of 2856cc was chosen: the claimed power output was 590bhp at 7900rpm, using a mechanical fuel injection pump.

The nose was filled with a vast petrol tank, and aluminum strengthening tubes as used in the 934 stiffened the nose area. Coil springs replaced the torsion bars all round, and there was a rear anti-roll bar which could be adjusted by the driver from the cockpit. The brakes were developed from those of the 917. The whole car, of course, was lightened quite considerably — so much so, in fact, that ballast was required to make it legal. Most of the non-structure panels were made from a fiberglass/polyurethane sandwich: these included the doors, engine cover, and the whole front wing section including both wings and the front spoiler/valance.

The first 935s featured massive rear wings, again supported on a box structure which also held the air-air intercooler, but at a race at Imola, this was decreed out of order by the scrutineers, so Porsche had to revert to water-air intercoolers, their radiators housed in the space in the rear fenders.

After a couple of races, too, the front fenders were modified in a way that the rule makers had most definitely *not* intended, but which was quite within the letter of the law. The regulations stated that fenders were free — they could be any size or shape. The intention was to allow wide flares, but Porsche took the FIA at their word — and chopped off the whole of the headlamp/fender top on each side. This gave better penetration and more downforce at the front, plus better stability in sidewinds. The headlights were incorporated into the front spoiler. The rule makers didn't like it, but they had to accept it!

The initial hassles over the inter-cooler, and the problems associated with the water-cooled system, took Porsche a while to overcome. Eventually, though, four victories, three seconds and three thirds plus a fifth, with Ickx and Mass doing most of the driving, gave Porsche the World Champion of Makes title for 1976.

Meanwhile, the third string to their bow was doing equally well. The Group 6 championship for 1976 was suddenly wide open when Alfa Romeo withdrew, leaving Renault, almost by default, as far and away the most likely winners.

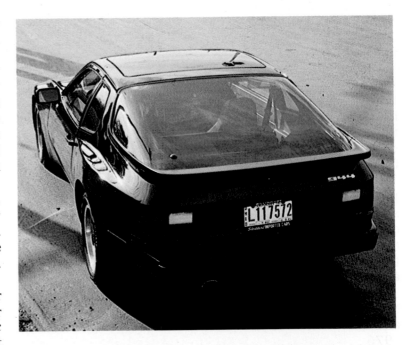

Right: A US-specification 1983 944 with more prominent fenders and repeater lights in the fenders. Below: The heavier bumpers are even more noticeable from the rear and a black paint finish cannot disguise them.

Fuhrmann made his decision: Porsche would go Group 6 racing as well. The go-ahead was given in September 1975, and the first car was being tested in February 1976.

The 936 combined the 917 with the 2.14-liter turbo engine. The space frame was longer and lower, but the 917 background was quite evident. Even the transaxles came from the 917. The 2.14-liter engine was chosen for the same reason as in 1974: the equivalency factor put it in the 3-liter class.

Porsche entered two 936s in 1976, sponsored by Martini, for the World Sports Car Championship. During secret testing before any racing was carried out the car was finished in a matt black color as a 'disguise,' though it fooled no one.

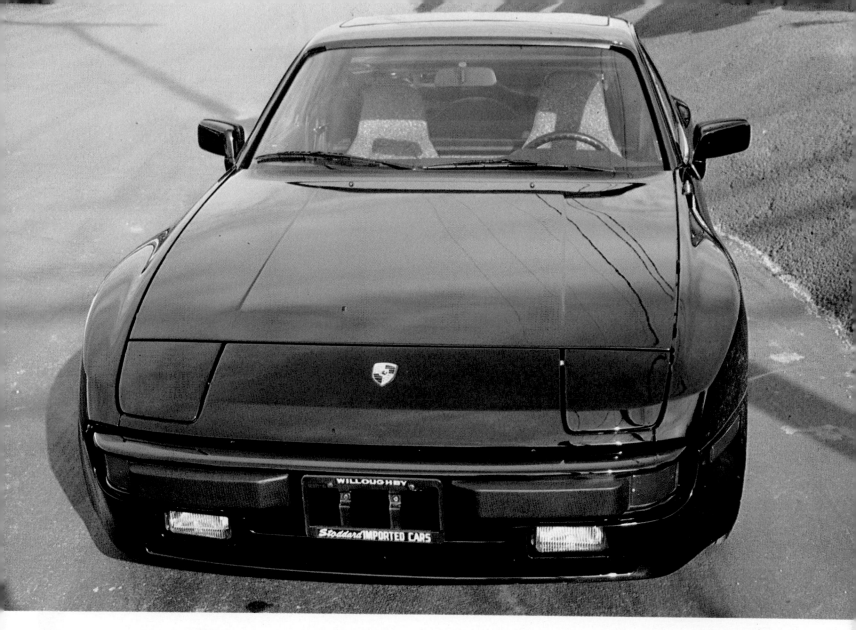

However, Count Rossi of Martini and Rossi, liked it, and for its first race at the Nurburgring it appeared in black but with the Martini stripes. However his color scheme didn't show up too well on the television cameras, so was abandoned from then on.

That Nurburgring race was the only one the 936 didn't win. For Le Mans a huge air intake/cooling scoop was installed behind and above the driver's head — but what needed cooling was his feet. With the low chassis the drivers sat much closer to assorted radiators with devastating results to their feet. Nevertheless the inevitable happened, and Ickx and van Lennep won.

For 1977 there were a few changes in the Group 5 rules. Norbert Singer, the man in charge of the 935 program, was an expert at interpreting rules — witness the new nose of the 1976 cars. He modified the 935 to produce the 935/77.

And so to 1982, for which FISA introduced a new category, Group C. This replaced the old Group 5 as the class around which the World Endurance Championship of Makes was based, and the 3-liter Group 6. Emphasis was placed on efficiency by restricting the amount of fuel a car could carry to 100 liters, and limiting the number of refueling stops a car can make in a given race.

Porsche jumped at the formula — they had been making excellent (at times spectacular) progress in improving their production car economy, and this was a way of showing the direction in which they felt motor racing should develop.

For the new formula, Porsche designed a (for them) radically new car. For a start it was the first racing Porsche to feature a monocoque chassis. The engine was the 2.6 Indy unit, which the Porsche engineers had worked over in the interests of better economy. At it's first outing at the now-traditional Silverstone 6 Hour meeting, in order simply to keep going, it was necessary to run at a slow pace. But the 956C, as the car was called, showed promise.

Backing up the three 956Cs of the factory at Le Mans were two more Category C Porsche-powered cars: one was a spaceframe car, powered by the 2.1-liter engine from Reinhold Jöst, the other an all-new car from Kremer, the C82. This used a 2.8-liter 935 engine, and featured the Kremer's own monocoque chassis.

The result is now history. For this, the 50th anniversary of the 24 hour race at the Sarthe circuit, Jacki Ickx, partnered by Derek Bell, won his sixth victory, and the 956s finished first, second and third. Two 935s followed them home, giving Porsche one of their best years ever.

Where now? The 924 and 944 are still in their early days of development and, like the 911, could go on to much greater things. So far Porsche have made no effort to place the 928 in competition, but its day, too, may come.

But probably the most exciting news is that Porsche are to provide the McLaren Formula 1 team with a turbocharged 1.5-liter power unit, rumored to be a water-cooled V6. Perhaps by the time you read this, a Porsche-powered car will have won another Grand Prix. Porscheophiles everywhere will smile with satisfaction, and perhaps with a touch of condescension — what else can be expected from Porsche but perfection?

Appendix

1948   Type 356 Prototype
Tubular chassis, mid-engined
Flat 4, 1131cc, 40bhp
Number made: 1
1950–1954   Type 356
Platform chassis, rear-engined
Flat 4, 1086cc, 40bhp (1950–1953)
Flat 4, 1286cc, 44bhp (Normal),
60bhp (Super)
Flat 4, 1488cc, 55bhp (Normal),
70bhp (Super)
Wheelbase: 82.7in
Number made: 7627
1955–1959   Type 356A
Platform chassis, rear-engined
Flat 4, 1286cc, 44bhp (Normal),
60bhp (Super)
Flat 4, 1488cc, 55bhp (Normal),
70bhp (Super)
Flat 4, 1582cc, 60bhp (Normal),
75bhp (Super)
Flat 4, 1498cc, 4 camshaft
100–110bhp (Carrera)
Flat 4, 1587.5cc, 4 camshaft,
105–115bhp (Carrera)
Wheelbase: 82.7in
Number made: 21,045

1959–1963   Type 356B
platform chassis, rear-engined
Flat 4, 1582cc, 60bhp (Normal),
75bhp (Super), 90bhp (Super 90)
Flat 4, 1966cc, 4 camshaft, 130bhp
(Carrera)
Wheelbase: 82.7in
Number made: 30,963
1963–1965   Type 356C
Platform chassis, rear-engined
Flat 4, 1582cc, 75bhp (C), 95bhp (SC)
Flat 4, 1966cc, 130bhp
Wheelbase: 82.7in
Number made: 16,668
1964–1969   Type 911 2 liter
Monocoque chassis, rear-engined,
Coupe or Targa
Flat 6, 1991cc, 130bhp (911),
160bhp (911S), 110bhp (911T),
140bhp (911E), 170bhp (911S
1968–1969)
Wheelbase: 87in (to 1968), 89.4in
thereon

1969–1971   Type 911 2.2 liter
Monocoque chassis, rear-engined,
Coupe or Targa
Flat 6, 2195cc, 125bhp (911T),
155bhp (911E), 180bhp (911S)
Wheelbase: 89.4in
1971–1973   Type 911 2.4 liter
Monocoque chassis, rear-engined,
Coupe or Targa
Flat 6, 2341cc, 130bhp (911T),
165bhp (911E), 190bhp (911S)
Wheelbase: 89.4in
1971–1977   Type 911 2.7 liter
Monocoque chassis, rear-engined,
Coupe or Targa
Flat 6, 2687cc, 210bhp (Carrera 2.7),
150bhp (911), 175 (911S),
Wheelbase: 89.4in
1975 to date   Type 911 3.0 liter
Monocoque chassis, rear-engined,
Coupe, Targa or Drophead
Flat 6, 2994cc, 200bhp (Carrera 3),
165bhp (911S), 180bhp (911SC)
Wheelbase: 89.4in
Number made: still in production
1965–1968, 1975   Type 912
Monocoque chassis, rear-engined,
Coupe or Targa
Flat 4, 1582cc, 90bhp (1965–1968),
1971cc, 90bhp (1975)
Wheelbase: 87in then 89.4in
Number made: 30,300 (1965–1968),
2099 (1975)

1975 to date   Type 911 Turbo
(Type 930)
Monocoque chassis, rear-engined,
Coupe
Flat 6, 2993cc, turbocharged, 260bhp
(1975–1977), 3299cc, 300bhp (1977
to date)
Wheelbase: 89.4in
Number made: still in production
1969–1971   Type 914/6
Monocoque chassis, mid-engined,
removable roof
Flat 6, 1991cc, 110bhp
Wheelbase: 96.5in
Number made: 3360
1976 to date   Type 924
Monocoque, front-engined, rear
wheel drive, Coupe
Straight 4, water-cooled, 1984cc,
125bhp (924), 177bhp (924 Turbo)
Wheelbase: 94.5in
Number made: still in production
1978 to date   Type 928
Monocoque, front-engined, rear wheel
drive, Coupe
V8, water cooled, 4474cc, 240bhp
V8, water cooled, 4664cc, 300bhp
(928S)
Wheelbase: 98.4in
Number made: still in production
1981 to date   Type 944
Monocoque, front-engined, rear wheel
drive, Coupe
Slant 4, water cooled, 2479cc, 163bhp
Wheelbase: 94.5in
Number made: still in production

RACING

1953–1956 Type 550
Ladder frame, mid-engined, Spyder
Laddr framed, mid-engined, Spyder and
Coupe (1956 space frame Type 550A)
Flat 4, 1488cc, 78bhp
Flat 4, 4 camshaft, 1498cc,
110–130bhp
**1956–1963   Type 718 RSK/RS60/
W-RS**
Space frame, mid-engined, Spyder
and Coupe
Flat 4, 1587cc, 150bhp
Flat 4, 1697cc, 165bhp
Flat 4, 1966cc, 165bhp
Flat 8, 1982cc, 210bhp
1959–1061   Type 718/2
Formula2/Formula 1
Space frame, mid-engined, single
seater
Flat 4, 1498cc, 155bhp

1962   Type 804 Formula 1
Space frame, mid-engined, single
seater
Flat 8, 1494cc, 180bhp
1964–1966   Type 904 Carrera GTS
Ladder box-section chassis, glassfiber
body bonded on
Flat 4, 1966cc, 180bhp
1966   Type 906 Carrera 6
Space frame, Coupe
Flat 8, 1991cc, 210bhp
1967–1968   Type 910
Space frame, Coupe and Spyder
Flat 6, 1991cc, 220bhp
Flat 8, 2196cc, 270bhp
1967–1968   Type 907
Space frame, Coupe and Spyder
Flat 6, 1991cc, 220bhp
Flat 8, 2196cc, 270bhp

1969–1971   Type 908
Space frame, Coupe and Spyder
Flat 8, 2997cc, 350bhp
1969–1973   Type 912
Space frame, Coupe and Spyder
Flat 12, 4494cc, 580bhp
Flat 12, 4905cc, 600bhp
Flat 12, 4998cc, 630bhp
Flat 12, 5374cc, 660bhp
Flat 12, turbocharged, 4494cc,
850bhp
Flat 12, turbocharged, 4998cc,
100bhp
Flat 12, turbocharged, 5374cc,
1100bhp
1976   Type 934
Monocoque, production based, Group 4
Flat 6, 2994cc, 330bhp

1976   Type 935
Monocoque, production based, Group 5
Flat 6, 2856cc, 590bhp
Flat 6, 2856cc, 630bhp (935/77)
Flat 6, 1425cc, 370bhp (935(2.0)
Flat 6, 3211cc, 750bhp (935/78)
1976–1981   Type 936
Space frame, Spyder, Group 6
Flat 6, 2143cc, 520bhp
Flat 6, 2143cc, 540bhp (936/77)
Flat 6, 2140cc, 580bhp (936/78)
Flat 6, 2560cc, 600bhp (936/81)
1982   Type 956
Monocoque, coupe
Flat 6, 2560cc, 600bhp+

Index

Acknowledgments

The author and the publishers would like to thank Nick Georgano, Bridget Daly and Richard Nichols for their help in editing the book, David Eldred who designed it and Ronald Watson who compiled the index.

Special credit is due to Nicky Wright who took most of the photographs, and to Charles Stoddard for allowing photographs to be taken of his unique collection of road and racing Porsches.

Thanks are due to the following who also supplied photographs:
Stoddard Imported Cars, Cleveland, pages 8, 9, 10, 11, 12, 13, 14, 18, 19.

We would also like to thank the following owners who kindly allowed their superb automobiles to be photographed for this book:
J Bailey (924 Turbo)
Jenny Branston (1973 914 4 cylinder)
David Edelstein (1958 356A)
M J Heudebourck (1979 911 SC Coupe)
Donald R Peterson (1958 356A Sunroof Coupe)
Norman Rogers (356B Roadster)
J Roulon-Miller (924 Turbo)
Mike Smith (1982 930 Turbo)
Dr L Stretton (1973 911E Coupe 2.4 liter)
Swinford Motors (1982 944)
Ray Wright (1955 356 Speedster)